AND
THEN
THE END
SHALL
COME

AND THEN THE END SHALL COME

Dale Rumble

Destiny Image Publishers
P.O. Box 310
Shippensburg, PA 17257
**"Speaking to the Purpose of God
for this Generation"**

ISBN 1-56043-063-X

For Worldwide Distribution
Printed in the U.S.A.

Acknowledgments

I wish to express special thanks to the following people:

Claudia Scott, of *Scott Info-Tech* for her work in typing, formatting and setting the manuscript.

Vera Brennan for editing the text.

My dear wife, Bertha, who is such a vital part of my ministry, for her prayers and personal encouragement.

This book is dedicated to all eleventh-hour laborers (Matthew 20:1-16).

Contents

Contents

Foreword

What sound are anointed ears, listening to the Spirit of God, hearing in this mighty hour? What is the prophetic direction of our generation as the sleeping Church comes alive and begins to move in power and authority? Dale Rumble has written a well delineated examination of **what, where, when** and **how** Kingdom authority is to flow from God's people to the world in communicating and demonstrating the Kingdom of God.

And Then the End Shall Come opens far more than an eschatalogical treatise of scripture. To a pastor of a local church, the message of this book can set the agenda for emphasis in equipping the saints for the work of the ministry. Dale Rumble's vision for ministry encompasses both local concerns and a far-reaching world view, both the present and the future, both here-and-now influence and the long awaited government of Christ to come.

This book is also filled with insights to equip the overcomer for inescapable tribulation. Rumble points to numerous facets of current spiritual deception raging in society with clear, profound accuracy, and then offers sound biblical strategy against the most subtle wickedness.

I confidently endorse *And Then the End Shall Come* as a manual on studying the Kingdom of God as the message of this hour in all its relevancy, truth and dynamic direction for the individual and the local church.

endorsement by

Earl Paulk, Bishop
Chapel Hill Harvester Church
Dacatur, Georgia

Introduction

I would like to introduce this book to readers as a road map of those major spiritual events that will lead to the Lord's return. It is a book with much information. However, information alone will not bring life. My prayer is that the Holy Spirit will speak through the words and impregnate hearts with a vision of the Lord's purpose for His Church in the closing days of this age of grace. I also pray that eyes will be opened to see the depths of deception and evil planned by satan. We should not be ignorant of these things!

Scripture states that the gospel of the Kingdom will be preached in the whole world as a final witness to all nations, and then the end shall come. This book reveals what the Kingdom and its gospel are. It also exposes the New Age Movement, which is designed to bring in a new world order.

Perilous times are coming upon the earth. Spiritual darkness and deception will increase. Political, economic and religious systems will be shaken.

But the glory and power of God will rest upon the Church, and the word for her is victory! As the Church submits to the government of Christ and He comes to have first place in everything, there will be a mighty harvest of souls brought into the Kingdom. The gospel of the Kingdom will bring a great demonstration of the grace of God. And then the end shall come!

Preface

What a privilege it is to serve the Lord today! We are living in the most exciting time ever in the history of the Church. These are days of great change, not only in the Church, but also in the arena of nations. It is difficult to fully grasp the significance of many events, and they are taking place at an accelerating rate! Who would have imagined how quickly communism would lose its control over nations in Europe? Who could have foreseen how Iraq, the greatest military force in Islam, would be humiliated and lose its power and armaments in a matter of days?

These are two new, immense fields that are being prepared by the Lord for the gospel. His promise that this gospel of the Kingdom would be preached in the whole world includes these nations. Therefore, our eyes need to be focused on the Lord as He prepares the Church for this final great task. She is entering into a mighty visitation of the Holy Spirit that will close this age.

The time of harvest has always existed; the fields have always been white for reaping. However, we are entering a unique period of time when the harvest of all harvests faces us. There are five ways in which this harvest differs from all previous ones.

- It involves not only a gathering of the grain, but is also the time when all tares will be gathered up to be burned (Matthew 13:24-30, 37-43).

- The time between reaping and sowing has been getting shorter, and now these activities will overlap (Amos 9:13).

- The level of lawlessness and sin in mankind will be greater than at any previous time in history (Jude 17-23, 2 Timothy 3:1-5, 2 Peter 3).

- The physical and spiritual state of many of those who make up the Lord's harvest will be that of great distress (Luke 14:16-24). Many will be hurting outcasts of society. This "discarded" human material the Lord will use to build His house. He delights to use warped boards, broken shingles and bent nails!

- This harvest will be the greatest demonstration of the grace of God in the history of the Church (1 Peter 1:13). It will be the final revelation of God's love to unsaved mankind before He comes to judge the nations and set up His Kingdom.

It has always been the Lord's will that His people have a burden to win the lost; it should be the lifestyle of every believer. Over the years various missionary and evangelistic endeavors have emerged as a result of visitations of the Holy Spirit. There have been those who have willingly laid down everything, including their own lives to take the gospel to those dying without Christ in foreign lands. However, there has not yet been a demonstration of the gospel that can compare to what is to come.

God has already begun to restore His Church. The increasing success of cell (or home) groups has enlarged the vision and changed the structure of many bodies; the growing presence and acceptance of spiritual gifts is making an impact on traditional churches. However, what lies ahead for the Church during this final awakening will be much greater in scope, for it is destined to touch the entire world. It will be **far more** comprehensive in its impact upon mankind. New dimensions of the power of God will be seen in spiritual warfare. Worldwide economic conditions, tribulations and persecutions will be unlike anything seen before. The true Church will be delivered from the bonds and structures that have tied her to the world. Bodies of believers will be knit together by flexible bonds of spiritual life and fellowship. There will be a great harvest of souls, primarily from among the poor, those deeply afflicted in the streets of sin, and from nations that have been closed to the gospel in the past. At the same time, there will occur a falling away of many in nominal Christendom because of demonic deception. The days ahead will not be like times of the past, and believers must prepare for them!

Over the years, human traditions and legalism have often been mixed with the gospel. This has diluted its message and power. A primary mark of this last move of God will be restoration of the gospel of the Kingdom. This is the message by which the Lord will establish His government in the Church. To this end, He has begun to judge and purify His people, for the present level of commitment and holiness are not adequate to contain the power that is to come. The fire of God is shaking and testing the quality of what exists in traditional Christianity. The smell of smoke will become common place! God can only use humble, broken men. The Church that is to emerge in the years ahead will be marked by godly integrity, accountable relationships and humility. And the glory of God will rest upon her! It will not only be a Church with restored truth, but it will also be a Church with great compassion and a burden to see lost souls brought to Christ. This age will close with a restored Church ministering a restored gospel: the gospel of the Kingdom!

CHAPTER ONE

What is the Kingdom?

Centrality of the King

To answer this question correctly, one must recognize that there is an absolutely central focus in the Kingdom of God: the King Himself! He is supremely important; His majesty, glory and will are always paramount! The Kingdom of God may be defined as that environment of subjects that **fully** manifests obedience to the will of the Lord. There has always been such a sphere, for God's Kingdom exists wherever He reigns. Thus, the Kingdom of heaven is also the Kingdom of God. When the Lord's prayer, "Thy kingdom come. Thy will be done on earth as it is in heaven," is answered, the earth will also be part of the Kingdom of God. This is a primary theme of the Bible. The Kingdom of God relates not only to spiritual things; every aspect of a believer's life should become subject to the Lord of lords and Kings of kings.

The Kingdom of God has always existed. It has no beginning or end, for it represents the sphere of God's domain. Since He created all life, He has always exercised dominion over a realm of His creatures. When satan and the angels that followed him, through the exercise of their free will, chose to disobey the Lord and go their own way, they could no longer be part of His Kingdom and were cast out.

Man and the Kingdom

When Adam was created, he was placed as a lord over the earth to rule and subdue this particular realm for God (Genesis 1:26-28). Adam lost this governmental authority and his righteous relationship with God because of his sin and disobedience, brought about through the deceptive, evil intervention of satan. The earth and its ecology, including mankind, then entered a new era. It began an age of death and decay under the demonic influence of satan, who had usurped control from Adam. Satan is appropriately called the god of this age.

Through compassion and mercy, God came to earth as a Savior to reclaim His inheritance in man. He took all our sin upon Himself, becoming sin for us and paying the price necessary to atone for our transgressions by dying in our place on the cross. He offers pardon freely to all men with an opportunity to return to Him. He invites us to come under the government of His Son, to be empowered with the Holy Spirit and to destroy the works of satan. We extend His Kingdom by making disciples of men and nations. Spiritual laws of the Kingdom are principles that bring moral and economic soundness to the nations that embrace them.

Through the new birth and indwelling Holy Spirit, the Kingdom is formed within every child of God. It is not a kingdom with a regimented lifestyle centered around legal constraints of behavior. It is a **divine** lifestyle in which Christ lives His life in us by the Spirit (Galatians 2:20). Kingdom theology is much more concerned with divine life than it is with divine knowledge. As we submit to His government, walking under the unction of the Holy Spirit, His laws become engraved in our hearts.

—For the kingdom of God is not eating and drinking, but **righteousness** *and* **peace** *and* **joy** *in the Holy Spirit.*

Romans 14:17

The proclamation of His gracious offer, along with prerequisites for the new birth and all commitments and promises, is communicated by the gospel of the Kingdom.

Truly, truly, I say to you, unless one is born of water and the Spirit, he cannot enter into the kingdom of God.

John 3:5

Kingdom Government

The Kingdom of God is **not a democracy**; there is only one will and one government present. His Kingdom is perfect, since God and His government are perfect. Thus, what we see of the Kingdom today always points toward a future glory and fullness. The Kingdom is not being built, nor is it maturing; it is **being extended.** In contrast, the Church is not perfect, since it is made up of imperfect individuals; however, it is being built toward a future maturity in Christ. The Church began on the day of Pentecost, while the Kingdom of God has always existed.

The Kingdom is extended whenever men respond to the gospel and submit themselves to His authority. The parables of the mustard seed and of the leaven that was hidden in meal both illustrate the principle of Kingdom extension (Matthew 13:31). The fact that the Lord's government is perfect does not mean that a newborn Christian will walk perfectly in the Spirit. Believers must learn to lay down their own wills in order to do His. Jesus is going to reign and subdue all enemies until He comes to have **first** place in everything (1 Corinthians 15:25, Colossians 1:18). All enemies of the cross are His enemies. Thus, Kingdom extension takes place within believers as they mature in Christ.

Once the Church is restored and purified, the Lord will return in Person with angelic hosts to gather His bride to Himself. With her, He will then vanquish the forces of evil, judge the nations and bring in the Millennium (Jude 14-15).

The center of everything in the Kingdom will **always** be the King Himself! All responsibility and government will **forever** rest upon Him (Psalm 145:13).

> —*And the government will rest on His shoulders; and His name will be called Wonderful Counselor, Mighty God, Eternal Father, Prince of Peace. There will be **no end to the increase of His government** or of peace*—.
>
> Isaiah 9:6b-7a

The Rebellion of satan

It would be totally inappropriate for the Lord and Creator of the universe to allow part of His creation to forever remain in rebellion against Him. His patience and longsuffering in dealing with sinful man is clearly evident in biblical history (Romans 9:22). In His Word, God has made known His purpose and strategy in reclaiming those whom He foreknew would belong to Him, to destroy all rebellion in the universe and to establish His Kingdom upon the earth.

All knowledge necessary for one to be saved and to fulfill the call of Christ is available in the Word of God. The Bible addresses the entire six thousand-year history of mankind from the day of Adam's creation.

Details of an earlier creation that may have existed at the time of satan's initial rebellion against God are largely unknown but, in any case, they are unessential to our salvation. Appropriate disciplines of science reveal that the earth is much older than six thousand years. God states that "in the beginning" He created the heavens and the earth. He points back to the immeasurable past of eternity, before the sun and moon were made to enable man to measure time. God's "day" in creation is not bounded by twenty-four hours.

Archaeological discoveries of fossil relics apparently depict an earlier creation that was different than that over which Adam was appointed ruler and custodian. It would appear the Lord placed satan at an earlier time as the cherub in charge of all creation including the earth (Ezekiel 28:14). Whether this was done to test the angelic beings we do not know. When satan sinned, he was cast out of the mountain of God's presence (Isaiah 14:12-14, Ezekiel 28:16). However, he first manifested a deceptive, corrupting influence within the sphere of his responsibility, deceiving many of the angels, leading them in rebellion against God. These fallen angels have become his representative authorities of evil in the heavens over specific cities and countries during this present age.

Satan's rebellion corrupted life on the earth at that earlier age. God apparently purged that evil with a judgment of water (2 Peter 3:5-6). Some Bible scholars[1] believe this judgment is implied in

Genesis 1:2 ("And the earth was formless and void"), with Genesis 1:3-26 describing God's recreation to prepare the earth for the day of Adam.

The Bible simply does not provide information of this earlier period of time, since it is not essential to the gospel of salvation. However, there are questions raised, the answers of which appear to have possible implications for this past era. One such question concerns the origin of demons. It would appear that demons are either the spirits of a pre-adamic race[1] or the spirits of offspring from unholy unions between certain fallen angels and women.[2] These particular fallen angels, who left their angelic state to have sexual relations with women, have been bound with chains in darkness awaiting judgment (Jude 6-7). It is a great sin when one order of created beings leaves the boundary of their nature to mingle with another order of created beings (Genesis 6:4). The apparent strategy of satan was to corrupt the seed of mankind and prevent the birth of those who would be heirs of the Kingdom, including even the birth of our Lord. Those born out of this ungodly union were giants in the land. They and their descendants were known by various names in Scripture: Nephilim, Anakim, Emim, Rephaim and Zamzummin. A primary reason God sent the flood was to destroy them. However, a later incursion took place (Numbers 13:33). This is why God instructed Joshua to "utterly destroy them" when Israel entered Canaan, a task that was not carried out fully (Joshua 11:21-22, 2 Samuel 21:16-22).

Demons are earthbound evil spirits that seek to indwell human beings (or even animals) in order to have bodies by which to express themselves. These two properties, being earthbound and seeking to indwell people, would indicate that demons are not fallen angels. Their mission is to induce sickness, suicide, oppression, depression and fear, and to entice people into specific sins such as lust, murder, hatred, perversion or addiction. They further seek to use their occultic powers to deceive anyone they can into believing that they represent God. They are satan's primary interface of evil influence in the world, operating under the direction of fallen angelic authorities in the heaven who are over cities, regions and countries.

Thus, the people of God are opposed by a hierarchical kingdom of wicked forces under the headship of satan, the god of this age. This is the sphere of spiritual opposition that stands against the Church.

*Because we are not wrestling against flesh and blood, but against the **rulers**, against the **authorities**, against the **rulers of the world**, of the darkness of this age, against the **spiritual powers of evil in the heavenlies**.*

Ephesians 6:12, IB

We Christians need to recognize that our ultimate goal is not to go to heaven; it is to rule with the King in His Kingdom. At the present time, a Christian's death does indeed mean going to be with the Lord in heaven. However, when the Lord Jesus returns, the Church will be caught up to be and to remain with the Lord. At that time, the saints will return with Him in His judgment of satan and the nations. Those who have proven to be overcomers will be given levels of authority to rule with Christ over the nations.

*And in the days of those kings the God of heaven will set up a kingdom which will never be destroyed, and that kingdom will not be left for another people; it will crush and put an end to all these kingdoms, but it **will itself endure forever**.*

Daniel 2:44

After the Millennium, the Lord God will come and dwell among His people on the earth (Revelations 21:1-3). Thus, our heart desire should focus on the King and the Kingdom He will establish upon the earth, not simply on going to heaven.

The Kingdom and Society Today

The impact of the traditional gospel message on society has been weak and deficient. This has been, in part, a result of some lost vital truths possessed by the early Church. Although much truth has been restored, there has not (apart from isolated instances, such as in China) been a restoration of the gospel of the Kingdom. In many instances, the gospel today has been reduced to simplistic formulae, such as "Just believe, and let Jesus come into your heart." There has not been a proper emphasis on calling sinners to deep heart repentance nor of the personal cost to become a disciple of the Lord. The goal of the gospel has been to escape hell or to be free from the problems of sin, rather than to embrace the Kingdom of God. The need of man has replaced the purpose of God in the gospel.

The following are three **significant** deficiencies of truth, the lack of which have been largely responsible for weakening the gospel ministry of modern churches:

- The lack of apostles and prophets to lay proper foundations for churches and impart the vision of God's purpose for the church.[3,4]

- The proper place of tribulation and trial in developing Christian character. The dispensational teaching of a pretribulation rapture[5] has built an escapist mindset in believers concerning the future, instead of encouraging them to heed God's Word to prepare for the tribulation that marks the end of this age. If we endure in our trials, we shall reign with Him; this is His promise to us (2 Timothy 2:11-12). This particular mindset has also encouraged the Church to be isolated from society rather than being a force for redemptive change.

- One of the first truths lost by the early Church, beginning with the teaching of Ignatius in the second century, was the fact that a local church is a spiritual organism, a local expression of the body of Christ in which **each** member is anointed to function in ministry. The teaching of Ignatius was largely responsible for the emerging of two classes of believers, clergy and laity. Over time the latter became spectators, with "valid" ministry being limited to a professional class of men qualified by education and ordained within a hierarchical order of leaders. The importance of God's anointing for charismatic spontaneity became secondary to teaching and dogma. To have a recognized ministry required one to become an ordained, full-time "clergyman." Anointed body ministry was thereby crippled, and man began to control what took place in church meetings. Secular trades and professions were seen as inappropriate for a man called into one of the five-fold ministries of Ephesians 4:11. These wrong concepts are still evident in the structure and ministry of contemporary church bodies today.

As a result of these and other areas of weakness, self-centered teaching has infiltrated the church. She has become inward focused instead of upward-looking. Budgets, programs, education, buildings, head

counts, doctrinal identity and personal ministry
status have become too important. Spiritual warfare
in evangelism, ministry to the poor, caring for the
aged and widows, establishing relationships that are
essential to the spiritual health of a church, and building unity between assemblies have been neglected.
Much of what social services do today in providing
care for people should be the work of the local church.

The years ahead will see a significant move of the
Holy Spirit in churches to bring ministry to the poor,
the street people and those in chains of addiction.
There will be revelation and grace given on how to
care for the poor and the aged. Ministries of the Spirit
will be given to many who will be called to function in
secular trades and professions. There will be a great
harvest of souls gathered in from people desperate in
their needs, for whom governments of the world have
no answer. There shall be a demonstration of the
power of God's salvation for those held in deep
bondage to sin. However, traditional concepts of ministry techniques alone will not accomplish this work.

We see even now the first signs of a new generation
of bond-servants being raised up to lead the Church
into the future. Society will once again hear prophets
speak to leaders and nations, pointing them to the
Kingdom of God. Apostolic teams will again lay proper
foundations for local churches. These will not be men
who dominate the sheep, but men who manifest the
gentle authority of servanthood. As God's power grows
within the Church, so will the fear of God return as it
was in the day of Ananias and Sapphira.

The arm of the Lord will restore His Church, equip
her with the gospel of the Kingdom, and through her
will bring light where there is darkness, health where
there is disease, victory where there is defeat, bread
where there is hunger, order where there is disorder,

life where there is death! A final revelation of the heart and power of God to the world will be manifested; and then the end shall come.

CHAPTER TWO

Kingdom Now or in the Future?

In the Beginning

The Kingdom of God is presented in Scripture as existing on earth today within and among those who belong to the Lord, but the Bible's emphasis is on a future greatness and glory of the Kingdom. We are to look for the Kingdom that is to come.

The starting point in understanding Kingdom chronology begins with the first man, Adam. My personal opinion concerning the possible thoughts of God at the time of Adam's creation are as follows: "I created lucifer to be the most beautiful and greatest of all angelic beings. I anointed and placed him as the covering cherub to oversee My creation, including the earth. However, because of pride, he rebelled against Me. Now, as I eternally planned, I shall take a portion of dirt from the earth he ruled over; I will breathe My Spirit in it and form a man to replace him. It will only be one man at first, but in the end I will bring forth an overcoming, many-membered man from his descendants who, under My Son, will rule over all creation. This man will not fail Me. His Kingdom will be established forever!"

The Nation of Israel

The next major step of the Lord after the fall of Adam was to establish a binding covenant between Himself and man that would become the basis of righteousness, commitment and relationship for all who would thereafter seek to have an inheritance in the Kingdom of God. This was accomplished in the covenant of faith made with Abraham. Because of this covenant and the place of faith in it, all true believers today are children of Abraham (Romans 4:13, Galatians 3:29).

From the descendants of Abraham, God formed the nation of Israel to whom He related primarily as a family and a nation. He called His people to be an earthly kingdom of priests serving Him in righteousness. They were to be unique and separate from all other people in the earth.

> *Now then, if you will indeed obey My voice and keep My covenant, then you shall be My own possession among all the peoples, for all the earth is Mine; and you shall be to Me a kingdom of priests and a holy nation.*
>
> Exodus 19:5-6

Just as satan had freedom to choose to serve or not to serve the Lord, so every individual in Israel was taught to personally love and serve the Lord God from his heart. It was not enough to simply be an Israelite by birth. God gave the law and ordinances through Moses so that each person could see and constantly be aware of the sinfulness of his heart (Romans 7:7-13, Galatians 3:17-19, 1 Timothy 1:9-11).

Through the prophets, God continually called His covenant people to repentance from the sin of going their own way. He promised future blessings if they would obey Him. One such important promise concerned the Messiah who would one day come to earth to be their King.

The prophet Daniel was given a vision concerning the future events that would lead to the coming of Messiah and the eventual establishing of His Kingdom on earth. Prior to the time of Daniel, there had been two great kingdoms among the nations of the world. The Egyptians, followed by the Assyrians.

The Lord revealed to Daniel that four more major kingdoms would arise among the nations before the fullness of God's Kingdom would be established on the earth (Daniel 2: 7-12). His vision addressed all that would come to pass prior to the Lord's first coming, as well as all that faces the people of God in the closing days of this age when the Lord will return to establish His Kingdom. These four kingdoms, which have been well documented in history, are the following:

- The (then current) kingdom of Babylon
- The Medo-Persian kingdom
- The kingdom of Greece
- The kingdom of Rome

The kingdom of Rome will become transformed into a powerful kingdom of spiritual evil at the end of this age. Scripture refers to this empire as Babylon (Revelation 17, 18). Counting this as one, seven major kingdoms will have arisen in the earth before the eighth and final one, the Kingdom of God, is established.

The End of the Age

The Roman kingdom, which has existed for over two thousand years, is highly pertinent to world affairs in the closing days of this age. It is characterized by the inability of nations to remain in union with one another, just as clay and iron do not adhere together (Daniel 2:40-43). This is reflected in the many divisions that are taking place between peoples because of ethnic factors such as race, language and customs. There is currently an intense drive for nationalism by groups that hitherto had been part of larger nations. This is very evident today in Yugoslavia and the Soviet Union who apparently will fragment into a group of independent countries.

During the last days of this fourth kingdom, probably from among a group of ten European nations, the man of lawlessness (the antichrist) will appear on the scene, and perilous times will cover the earth. He will bring forth a kingdom of deception and evil with great power and influence in fields of politics, commerce and religion. He will seek to establish a new world order. This is destined to end in great tribulation, the time of satan's wrath.

However, it will also be a time of purifying and purging the people of God so they will be able to stand victoriously in the great spiritual warfare of that time, and be made ready to inherit the Kingdom prepared for them.

> *And some of those who have insight will fall, in order to refine, purge, and make them pure, until the end time—.*

Daniel 11:35

The apostle Paul pointed to tribulation as preceding the establishment of God's Kingdom on earth.

*—strengthening the souls of the disciples, encouraging them to continue in the faith, and saying, "**Through many tribulations** we must enter the kingdom of God."*

Acts 14:22

It was revealed to Daniel that the Kingdom which the Lord sets up will include peoples from **all** nations, not just Israel. Those of His people who have insight, who prove faithful and overcome, will rule with the Lord in His Kingdom.

—And behold, with the clouds of heaven One like a Son of Man was coming—and to Him was given dominion, glory and a kingdom, that all the peoples, nations and men of every language might serve Him. His dominion is an everlasting dominion which will not pass away; and His kingdom is one which will not be destroyed.

Daniel 7:13b-14

Daniel was given some understanding of the spiritual conflict the saints would face in those days.

I kept looking, and that horn [the antichrist] was waging war with the saints and overpowering them until the Ancient of Days came, and judgment was passed in favor of the saints of the Highest One, and the time arrived when the saints took possession of the kingdom.

Daniel 7:21-22

*Then the sovereignty, the dominion, and the greatness of all the kingdoms under the whole heaven will be given to the people of the saints of the Highest One; His kingdom will be an everlasting kingdom, and **all the dominions will serve and obey Him.***

Daniel 7:27

The Messiah

It was during the early years of the Roman Empire, when it was at its peak, that the promised Messiah, the Christ of God, came to earth to proclaim and establish His Kingdom. He went first to Israel, His covenant people, since to them belonged the promised blessings of the Kingdom. It was theirs on the basis of heritage and election. However, they would not receive Him. Rabbinical Judaism did not grasp the prophetic significance of God's promises made to them concerning their Messiah. The religious leaders of Israel rejected their Lord and had Him crucified.

The Kingdom was then taken from Israel and offered to those who would serve and obey Him. Jesus made this clear to the leaders of Israel in His parable of the landowner who planted a vineyard and rented it out to vinegrowers before going on a journey (Matthew 21:33-44). His key words to the Pharisees are found in verse 43:

> *Therefore I say to you, the kingdom of God **will be taken away from you,** and be given to a nation producing the fruit of it.*

During the Old Testament era, Israel's instruction was centered in the law and the prophets; when Jesus came, God's message was the gospel of His Kingdom (Luke 16:16). God began to speak to His people through His Son. This gospel brought entirely new dimensions of understanding to the people concerning the purpose of God and the nature of His Kingdom. Demons were cast out, the sick were healed, the dead were raised and the gospel was preached to the poor and crippled (Matthew 4:23). As these miracles took place, the people were told that the Kingdom of God had come to them (Matthew 12:28, Luke 10:9). The power of satan was broken in the lives of those who received the Lord's words with faith and repentance. The leaders of Israel were looking for a king to reign over them and free them from Roman rule. However, the Lord ministered and demonstrated the life and power of a spiritual Kingdom. He recognized that it was satan, not Rome, who was the real enemy. He continually pointed the crowds and His disciples to the state and attitude of their hearts, for it is here that He would lay the foundation for His Kingdom.

*But seek **first His kingdom and His righteousness;** and all these things shall be added to you.*

Matthew 6:33

The Kingdom can not be extended or maintained by activities of the flesh. Only the Spirit of the Lord can do this. The key for believers is to recognize that no good thing dwells in their flesh and that Kingdom life is a matter of faith, humility and purity of heart. Meekness had, up to this time, been seen as a sign of weakness; now it came to be recognized as strength under discipline. The gospel of Jesus declared that the meek would inherit the earth. Meekness and humility became essential qualities of those who would inherit the Kingdom to come. How desperately the Church today needs to obey His words!

Come to Me, all who are weary and heavy-laden, and I will give you rest. Take My yoke upon you, and learn from Me, for I am gentle and humble in heart; and you shall find rest for your souls.

Matthew 11:28-29

Whoever then humbles himself as this child, he is greatest in the kingdom of heaven.

Matthew 18:4

The climax of Christ's gospel was not His words, but His demonstration of God's love when He suffered death on the cross; then, taking the keys of Hades and death, He broke the power of satan in His resurrection. What looked like defeat and weakness was really the power of God bringing salvation! He stripped satan of his power, shaming him and making a public spectacle of him.

The cross of Christ is the way of His Kingdom!

The Kingdom and Israel

There is both a spiritual and a natural dimension in what God is doing in the earth today. The spiritual dimension concerns the Church, her restoration and her preparation for the Lord's return. In this context, it is correct to state that **every** man is either in Adam or in Christ. One is either saved or he is not. There is no third option. The seed of Abraham was promised to be as "stars of the heaven." This refers to those who have received the promise of the Spirit by faith and who make up the Church. All national or racial identities cease to have significance in the body of Christ.

There is neither Jew nor Greek, there is neither slave nor free man, there is neither male nor female; for you are all one in Christ Jesus.
Galatians 3:28

The eyes of the Church turn upward to the city of the living God, which is the mother of all who live by faith.

But the Jerusalem above is free; she is our mother.
Galatians 4:26

But you have come to Mount Zion and to the city of the living God, the heavenly Jerusalem, and to myriads of angels, to the general assembly and church of the first born—.
Hebrews 12:22-23a

However, the Spirit of God is also doing a work that concerns natural Israel. He is bringing Jews back from all the nations to which they had been scattered. They are coming with unseeing eyes and closed hearts, and more are destined to return according to prophecies in the Old Testament. As this age comes to a close, the Spirit of God will lift the veil from a remnant of those who make up the nation of Israel and they will be saved, becoming part of the Church. This will apparently be one of the very last visitations of the Lord before He pours out His wrath and judgment. Some believers, having a burden for Israel, are preparing themselves today to play a role in this visitation.[6]

> *But whenever they persecute you in this city, flee to the next; for truly I say to you, you shall not finish going through the cities of Israel, until the Son of Man comes.*
>
> Matthew 10:23

> *For I do not want you, brethren, to be uninformed of this mystery, lest you be wise in your own estimation, that a partial hardening has happened to Israel until the fullness of the Gentiles has come in—.*
>
> Romans 11:25

When the Lord returns to judge the nations, He will have great wrath and many will die in His judgment. Apparently, one third of the nation of Israel will survive (Zechariah 13:8-9). This remnant will recognize their Messiah and be saved, being born again, as it were, in a day (Matthew 23:37-39, Zechariah 12:9-14). Israel will then enter the Millennium having a unique place among those who survive from the other nations. It is likely that they will be much like believers are today, a natural people possessing the Holy Spirit, who will live on a renewed earth (Isaiah 65:17-23). Israel will then inherit the natural promises made to them concerning their land. This will include not only the land of Canaan possessed by the tribes under Joshua, but also all the land from the Euphrates River to the Nile in Egypt (Genesis 15:18-21). They will be Abraham's seed who were to be as the sand of the sea.

The Lord will reign with His Church in the New Jerusalem, and there will be a special interface to the other nations through Jerusalem in Israel (Zechariah 14:16-21).

All nations will be tested when satan is released at the end of the Millennium. After a final judgment, the Lord will then establish His Kingdom in its fullness upon the earth.

Restoration of Truth

After the ascension of Jesus, the gospel of the Kingdom continued to be the message of the first apostles and the early Church. However, in the second century there began a great falling away of truth that continued until the Dark Ages had enveloped Europe.

Since the days of Martin Luther, there has been a progressive restoration of major truths. This process of restoration has accelerated during the present century, and numerous assemblies have now arisen in which gifts and ministries of the Holy Spirit are present and where men of God seek to build churches after the pattern of the early Church (Acts 3:19-21).

In concert with this restoration, the Lord is bringing fresh revelation of His purpose for the Church in the closing days of this age and of the role and importance of the gospel of the Kingdom.

The years ahead will see a significant impact of the Church in societies of the world. However, traditional methods will prove inadequate. There must arise the many-membered body of Christ, the true Church under His government through whom the Lord will do a great end-time work. His plan is a restored Church with a restored gospel. Let us examine what Scripture has to say concerning the gospel of the Kingdom with which the Lord will bring this age to a close.

CHAPTER THREE

The Gospel of the Kingdom

The Beginning and the End

The particular period of time in which we live today, referred to as the Church Age, began when, empowered by the Holy Spirit, the Lord Jesus commenced His earthly ministry by preaching the gospel of the Kingdom (Matthew 9:35).

> *And Jesus was going about in all Galilee, teaching in their synagogues, and proclaiming the* **gospel of the kingdom,** *and healing every kind of disease and every kind of sickness among the people.*
>
> Matthew 4:23

The gospel He preached became the commission He later gave to His disciples (Matthew 10:5-10, Mark 16:15-18). It was also the gospel preached by the early Church (Acts 19:8, 20:25, 28:23, 31; Romans 15:18-19).

In fact, the gospel of the Kingdom is the **only** gospel ever given to the Church. There is not one gospel for the unsaved and another for the Church; everyone is called to come under the government of God. It is as simple as that, for the gospel of the Kingdom is designed to establish God's government on earth, beginning in the Church.

Scripture declares that there is one Spirit, one body, one faith and one hope of our calling (Ephesians 4:4-5). This statement is true because there is **only one gospel!** However, during its nineteen centuries the Church has become fragmented into many bodies with individual groups emphasizing distinct aspects of the gospel. The following are current examples of such "gospels": the social gospel, dispensationalism, the full gospel, liberation theology, dominion theology, faith and prosperity, the gospel of liturgy. Each emphasis is a focus on some doctrine or need that has been viewed as essential truth. However, the gospel of the Kingdom has but one objective: to accomplish the purpose of God by establishing His government in men's lives. As this is accomplished, the needs of those who respond will be met. They shall be abundantly satisfied, but within the context of His government in their lives.

In these days of restoration, as the Church is being prepared for tribulation, conflict and a great, final ingathering of souls, the Lord is once again bringing the gospel of His Kingdom into focus. It is the ministry and message destined to **close this age of grace, even as it opened it.**

*And this **gospel of the kingdom** shall be preached in the whole world for a witness to **all the nations, and then the end shall come.***
                                    Matthew 24:14

To most people, the gospel is God's good news of His provision to forgive them of all sin and bring them into His Kingdom. However, the gospel of the Kingdom is more comprehensive than that. It is to bring us into His Kingdom **and** to build us together on the foundation of His Son so that we become an expression of His Kingdom upon the earth. In other words, we are **brought into** the Kingdom to **become established** under His government. The gospel concerns the purpose of God as well as the needs of sinful men.

God is not looking for members in the sense of building an organization; He wants us to **know** Him as our Father, One whose arms are outstretched toward us in love, whose heart's desire is that we become established in Jesus and share His glory (Ephesians 3:17-19).

> *Now to Him who is able to **establish you** according to my gospel and the preaching of Jesus Christ—.*

Romans 16:25a

> *And it was for this He called you through our gospel, that you might **gain the glory of our Lord Jesus Christ.***

Second Thessalonians 2:14

If the intent in preaching the gospel is only to save men from hell, its message will be limited. However, the lost are not only invited to be justified by faith and freed from **sin and judgment,** but they are also **called to inherit the life of God and be part of His Kingdom.**

> *Therefore having been justified by faith, we have peace with God through our Lord Jesus Christ—and we exult in hope of the glory of God.*

Romans 5:1-2b

The following nine subheadings reveal characteristics of the gospel of the Kingdom. Although each one
does not carry equal importance, all are necessary to
accurately express the heart and purpose of God
through the gospel.

(1) The Gospel and the Holy Spirit

There can be no gospel apart from the Holy Spirit.
Scripture reveals that the gospel involves the following **three** major works of the Spirit in the lives of
those who do respond to its message.

- The forgiveness of sins and restoration of a personal relationship with God through faith in the
  death, burial and resurrection of Jesus. The
  Kingdom of God is a spiritual Kingdom. To enter,
  one must be born of the Spirit. Clearly, the
  gospel message and the ears of hearers must be
  spiritually anointed for this to take place.

- Victory over satan and his hosts in spiritual
  warfare.

- A victorious, fruitful life as a living stone in the
  house of God in matters pertaining to character,
  relationship and service.

None of these supernatural works can take place
apart from a deep work by the Holy Spirit in the
hearts of men.

Jesus did not begin to preach the gospel until
He had **first** received fullness of the Holy Spirit
(Matthew 3:16-17, Luke 3:21-22).

The early disciples were charged by Jesus not to
begin their ministry of witness **until** they were baptized with the Holy Spirit (Acts 1:4-8).

The emphasis of the Holy Spirit in the gospel, as
in all ministry, is to glorify and exalt the Lord Jesus,

pointing hearers to His finished work on the cross. The gospel is referred to in scripture as the "gospel of the glory of Christ" (2 Corinthians 4:4). It is when men lose sight of the centrality of Jesus that they begin to preach other gospels.

Some would limit the anointing of the Spirit to quickening gospel messages on repentance and the new birth and to performing attesting signs to confirm the spoken word. However, when we examine the ministry of Jesus and the anointing that rested upon Him, we realize that it encompassed much more.

Isaiah speaks of His anointing as follows:

*The Spirit of the Lord is **upon me,** because the Lord has **anointed me** to bring good news—.*

Isaiah 61:1

*And the Spirit of the Lord will rest on Him, the spirit of **wisdom** and **understanding,** the spirit of **counsel** and **strength** [might], the spirit of **knowledge** and the **fear of the Lord.***

Isaiah 11:2

When one considers the above six distinct characteristics listed in Isaiah 11 concerning the anointing resting upon Jesus, it becomes quite apparent that the gospel He preached was more than sermons on repentance and the forgiveness of sins. It also included a personal demonstration of God's love and grace ministered with divine wisdom, understanding, counsel, power and knowledge. He sought to bring lost men into a **full** and **complete** salvation that included His lordship over their lives. He wanted them free in body, soul and spirit from all other dominions in order to belong **totally** to Him. The same anointing is needed today to be effective in preaching the gospel. If the gospel of the Kingdom were truly preached, churches would spend far less time on counseling, resolving personal issues and healing relationships.

One can recognize examples of these six aspects of Christ's anointing from Scripture.

- The spirit of wisdom — When the woman taken in the act of adultery was brought before Jesus, there were witnesses of her sin. Because of these witnesses, Jesus was unable to minister mercy to her. Therefore, He said nothing and waited for the Spirit of God to give Him a word of wisdom.

He who is without sin among you, let him be the first to throw a stone at her.

John 8:7

Through divine wisdom, Jesus was then able to minister mercy and forgiveness to her; it became a doorway for the gospel.

- The spirit of understanding — This is seen most clearly in His understanding of **who** He was and **why** He had come into the world. **Everything** He did came from His understanding the purpose of His Father. The gospel He ministered and the life He lived were based on principles of the cross even though His words looked forward to Calvary. Everyone who embraces the gospel also has a cross to pick up and carry.

And he who does not take his cross and follow after Me is not worthy of Me. He who has found his life shall lose it, and he who has lost his life for My sake shall find it.

Matthew 10:38-39

- The spirit of counsel — Whenever Jesus gave counsel or advice, either to individuals or to groups, He presented truth so that **only** those whose hearts were open and receptive would respond. Others would simply not understand. The parables He taught are a good example of this (Matthew 13:3-17, 34-35; John 8:43). Jesus never ministered situation ethics or general principles; His words were spirit and life directly into the hearts of those to whom He spoke. His words were God's *KERUGMA* (God's proclamation); they were not negotiable, nor could they be debated.

- The spirit of strength — The spirit of strength is clearly manifested by His mighty miracles, especially those that demonstrated His power over death.

- The spirit of knowledge — This anointing was evident in the many instances when, by a word of knowledge, He acted according to what was in the hearts of men. His words and actions were **always** directed by what He saw in the hearts of His audience. Jesus recognized that the gateway for the gospel lay in the human heart; it is no different today.

- The spirit of the fear of the Lord — Jesus demonstrated an explicit humility by speaking and doing **only** those things He was commanded to by His Father. He did **nothing** on His own initiative. To mix one's own strategy, doctrine or emphasis with the gospel will dilute and weaken it. The fear of God will keep this from happening. This is not fear of His judgment, but fear of displeasing and misrepresenting Him. Jesus **always** honored and pleased His Father.

These six aspects of the anointing upon Jesus make it abundantly clear that one cannot preach the gospel of the Kingdom apart from gifts and anointings of the Holy Spirit. Indeed, if spiritual manifestations of power, discernment, knowledge, wisdom and humility are not present, one's ministry will not reveal Christ to those who are in bonds of deception.

Jesus is the Way, the Truth and the Life. He is the **only** Door to eternal life. He came, first of all, to reveal the Father to mankind; and second, He came to lay down His life to reconcile men back to the Father. This is what He was anointed to accomplish. His gospel was far more than the words He spoke. It included **all** that took place, both word and deed, in His relationship with men, women and children. Thus, it is the **total** record of His life, His teaching and acts, including the cross, that makes up the gospel He ministered.

For this reason, the beatitudes in particular provide a significant portion of the gospel. For they are not only words of truth, but they also express the very essence of Kingdom life. They are a body of truth that the Lord is calling His people to receive fresh understanding of today. They are **essential** to establishing His Kingdom. They point to the cross as the basis for life and government in God's Kingdom. Thus, the following are **vital** excerpts from the gospel of the Kingdom:

- *Blessed are the poor in spirit—.*
- *Blessed are the meek—.*
- *Blessed are the merciful—.*
- *Blessed are the pure in heart—.*
- *Blessed are the peacemakers—.*
- *Let your light shine before men in such a way that they may—glorify your Father who is in heaven.*
- *Love your enemies and pray for those who persecute you.*

- *Whoever then humbles himself as this child, he is greatest in the kingdom of heaven.*

- *Whoever wishes to become great among you shall be your servant.*

- *For I was hungry, and you gave Me something to eat; I was thirsty and you gave Me drink; I was a stranger and you invited Me in; naked, and you clothed Me; I was in prison, and you came to Me.*

Each of the above teachings reflects life, relationship, ministry and government in the Kingdom of God. Those who proclaim and practice these virtues are the ones who will rule in the Kingdom. There is no place in the gospel of the Kingdom for covetousness, pride, competition or jealousy to exist. However these are present in the church today. The need of believers is not higher self-esteem, as some would teach; our true need is for genuine humility and repentance.

For too long, we have disassociated such verses from the gospel. However, they represent the very truths that make our witness become the light of the world and the salt of the earth. These spiritual laws and principles should be visibly present in the lives of those preaching the gospel of the Kingdom, for they reflect the government of God. They are the truths that bring righteousness and prosperity to society. We are called to be witnesses of Christ; what we stand for must be both **heard and seen** by those to whom we appeal. For example, do we have grace to love those who persecute and hate us?

The Holy Spirit is a Person, and one cannot accept His acts without also accepting His character and priorities. For too long, believers have sought to have His deeds of power among them but have not equally desired to walk in the integrity of His ways; this has limited the gospel.

(2) The Gospel of the Kingdom is a Proclamation of Divine Simplicity

When the gospel is presented to lost men, its message and spirit will be masked if it is made complicated and difficult to understand. The simplicity of the gospel lies in the anointing of the Holy Spirit. The love of God does not require a special vocabulary with which to be expressed; it is easily understood by the simple when it is offered in word and deed.

> *Truly I say to you, whoever does not receive the kingdom of God like a child shall not enter it at all.*

Luke 18:17

The heart of the gospel is not a message of reformation, nor does it define righteous conduct. It is an invitation to eternal life in the Kingdom of God. The gospel of the Kingdom is absolutely transparent to earthly cultures and race. To embrace the gospel is to become a son of God in His Kingdom, a new order and culture of the Spirit. We are part of a new man. We may retain evidences of our culture in this life, but after the resurrection even this will disappear.

The gospel proclaims God's **unconditional** love for lost mankind, and it proclaims the **total, complete** and **absolute** victory of the Lord Jesus over satan, sin and death through His death and resurrection. It is a proclamation that **everything** necessary to bring the lowest sinner from the domain of darkness into the Kingdom of God's beloved Son has been provided in the all-sufficient work of the cross. Furthermore, **all** that a convert requires to walk in victory over sin is available **through faith** in what

Christ has purchased by His death, burial and resurrection.

The **two** conditions that men must meet to receive eternal life are **faith and repentance.** The power of the gospel is hindered whenever the need for repentance is not emphasized, or when simplicity in the gospel message is lost. Because it is simple, the gospel can be understood in the heart of a child or one whom the world would consider to be a fool (Isaiah 35:8, 1 Corinthians 1:26-28).

Simplicity of faith, rather than education, is the basis of understanding all mysteries of the Kingdom. In the first place, they cannot be grasped through human intelligence; they must be revealed by the Spirit. As we know Him, so will we know the secrets of His Kingdom.

> —*To you it has been granted to know the mysteries of the kingdom of God, but to the rest it is in parables, in order that seeing they may not see, and hearing they may not understand.*
>
> Luke 8:10

(3) A Threefold Divine Witness Marks the Gospel of the Kingdom

Salvation is both an experience of passing from death into life and of receiving a threefold witness that the life of the Son will enable one to overcome the world.

> *And who is the one who overcomes the world, but he who believes that Jesus is the Son of God? This is the one who came by **water** and **blood,** Jesus Christ; not with the water only, but with the water and with the blood. And it is the **Spirit** who bears witness, because the Spirit is the truth. For there are **three** that bear witness, the **Spirit** and the **water** and the **blood;** and*

*the three are in agreement—. The one who believes in the Son of God has the **witness in himself**—and the witness is this, that God has given us eternal life, and this life is in His Son.*

First John 5:5-8, 10-11

First, the Spirit bears witness in the new birth that the blood of Christ has cleansed away all sin. Second, in water baptism He bears witness that our sinful, carnal nature , which was crucified with Christ on the cross, has been cut away by spiritual circumcision and buried in the waters of baptism.

I have been crucified with Christ—.

Galatians 2:20a

*Therefore we have been **buried** with Him **through baptism** into death, in order that as Christ was raised from the dead through the glory of the Father, so we too might walk in **newness of life.** —knowing this, that our **old self was crucified** with Him, that our body of sin **might be done away with,** that we should no longer be slaves to sin—.*

Romans 6:4,6

*And in Him you were also **circumcised** with a circumcision made without hands, in the removal of the body of the flesh by the circumcision of Christ; **having been buried with Him in baptism**—.*

Colossians 2:11-12a

Third, the Holy Spirit bears witness that we are raised up from the waters of baptism with power to walk in newness of life because of His abiding presence in us, a life in the Spirit that overcomes the world.

By faith, we reckon that through the death, burial and resurrection of Christ, because of our identification with Him through His blood, water baptism and the Spirit, we are now dead to sin. We simply **do not** have to sin! We have, by faith, exchanged our old sinful life for His glorious new life, a life which He now lives within us.

This is the basis of Kingdom life. It is how converts are to be brought into the Kingdom (1 Corinthians 15:3-4). It is how the government of God is introduced into the lives of new believers. Those who baptize others should recognize that by the authority in the Name of the Lord a vital work of the Spirit takes place in the hearts of those being immersed.

The pattern of salvation is pictured in the exodus of Israel from Egypt (Exodus 12-14). First, the **blood** was placed on the door posts. Second, the Egyptian army and oppressors of the Lord's people were swallowed up in the **waters** of the Red Sea; and thirdly, the Israelites were led by the **pillar of cloud and fire** toward the Promised Land. Blood, water and Spirit!

The first sermon preached in the early Church pointed to this threefold witness. It took place on the day of Pentecost after the Holy Spirit had been poured out upon the first disciples (Acts 2:1-38). To explain what happened, Peter preached to the multitude of onlookers explaining who Jesus was and why He had died a substitutionary death for them. The people believed his words and, being pierced to the heart, they asked what they should do in response. Peter's answer to them pointed to God's threefold provision:

> *Repent [i.e. because you have believed], and let each of you be baptized in the name of Jesus Christ for the forgiveness of your sins; and you shall receive the gift of the Holy Spirit.*
>
> Acts 2:38

God's witness to the gospel is greatly hindered, or eliminated altogether, when ministers are not faithful to preach the whole truth. When the blood of Christ is not properly emphasized, when water baptism is presented as an option instead of a command so that there is no faith for immediate immersion, by baptizing without expecting anything to take place in the heart of the candidate, when converts are put on probation to see if their salvation is valid before water baptism, or when converts are not exhorted to be baptized in the Holy Spirit as soon as they have repented and believed the gospel, the work of the Lord is hindered. The threefold witness is a **vital** support and **foundation** to all who repent and believe the gospel of the Kingdom.

(4) The Gospel of the Kingdom Proclaims the Grace of God

By grace, God apprehends individuals to be ambassadors of His mercy and to proclaim the gospel of His Kingdom. The life of Paul exemplified this truth (1 Corinthians 15:10).

*But I [Paul] do not consider my life of any account as dear to myself, in order that I may finish my course, and the ministry which I received from the Lord Jesus, to testify solemnly of the **gospel of the grace** of God.*

Acts 20:24

By grace the gospel of grace is proclaimed, so that sinners can be saved by the grace of God. There is absolutely nothing that we can contribute to our salvation except to believe and repent—even faith is a gift of God. It is altogether a matter of grace (John 1:16; Romans 3:23-25, 5:20-21; Ephesians 1:3-7, 2:4-9)!

*For if by the transgression of the one [i.e. Adam], death reigned through the one, much more those who receive the **abundance of grace** and of the **gift of righteousness** will reign in life through the One, Jesus Christ.*

Romans 5:17

*For the wages of sin is death, but the **free gift** of God is eternal life in Christ Jesus our Lord.*

Romans 6:23

God has foreknown every detail of our lives since long before we were born. Therefore, He knows the measure of grace we will need as believers to fulfill our call in Him. This grace, which has been prepared from the beginning of time, is made available to us when we are born of His Spirit, and it is **sufficient** for every need we have, regardless of past mistakes and failures.

*—who has saved us, and called us with a holy calling, not according to our works, but according to **His own purpose and grace** which was granted us in Christ Jesus **from all eternity.***

Second Timothy 1:9

We are not to be preoccupied with the failures and mistakes of our past life before we came to Christ. Our eyes are to be upon Him and on the grace He extends to us, for that will be sufficient for us to fulfill our call, regardless of misguided decisions in the past. Neither are we to see ourselves as limited in our call by physical handicaps. We are called with a holy calling, one that is accompanied by all the grace we will ever need; and this grace surpasses all failures of the past and weaknesses of the present. His strength is made perfect in our weakness.

"—My grace is sufficient for you, for [My] power is perfected in weakness!" Most gladly, therefore,

I will rather boast about my weaknesses, that the power of Christ may dwell in me.

Second Corinthians 12:9

We are His workmanship, created in Christ for works prepared beforehand for us to walk in, and for which grace has been provided for us (Ephesians 2:10). We are always to be faithful and obedient, but victory is never a question of our ability; it is altogether a matter of His anointing and grace (Romans 12:6; Ephesians 4:7, 11). God seeks to be seen and glorified in our lives and ministry. He builds His house with what society discards. Our handicaps and weaknesses become the basis of His grace in our lives. All must then recognize that it truly is God who does the work, and He receives the glory. This is the reason why not many noble, or strong, or wise in the eyes of the world become partakers of God's grace. They do not see their need. The key virtue is humility; as long as we are small in our own eyes, God can and will use us. We cannot and we must not ever depend upon our own strength; we are to be strong in the grace of God and rest in Him!

There is an aspect of God's grace that relates to time and place. For example, the grace of God visited the nation of Israel when Jesus began His ministry of the gospel of the Kingdom. After His ascension, the grace of God was then extended to gentile nations. In periods of revival, there have been times of significant manifestations of grace in various localities and nations. However, the coming ministry of the gospel of the Kingdom over all the world will demonstrate the **greatest** measure of God's grace ever to be seen on earth! This is what many current prophetic words on church restoration and world evangelism are pointing to; this will be the time when the bride of Christ prepares herself for her Lord's return and when a number from Israel will come into the Church by

God's grace. Our eyes and hearts are to be focused on **Him** as He reveals His Person and purpose for these last days. Peter expressed it well:

*Therefore, gird your minds for action, keep sober in spirit, fix your hope **completely on the grace** to be brought to you at the revelation of Jesus Christ.*

First Peter 1:13

We cannot look at past visitations and conditions alone to understand what lies ahead, for the future will involve new dimensions of God's power and grace, as well as great manifestations of evil and tribulation. It will be unlike anything ever seen on earth before (Matthew 24:4-14, 21-24; Isaiah 60:1-5; Haggai 2:6-9; Joel 2:30-32, 3:13-17). All things are under the control of our Lord, and He will do a new thing in the earth. There is great sin in the cities of our land, but there is more grace available than there is sin. Therefore, our eyes must be on Him and upon the grace He extends to us. We are not to anticipate the future on the basis of what has happened in the past (Isaiah 43:18-21). We must be like Noah, who built for unheard of times and conditions which he had never before seen or experienced. Like Noah, we are to move in obedient faith. Grace teaches us how to live in the present and look to the future (Titus 2:11-14).

Grace brings with it a responsibility of obedience; we are not to remain the same as we have always been. The past charismatic renewal illustrates this point. The Lord manifested His grace in pouring out the Holy Spirit on many denominations. This blessing was bestowed so that there would be change. While this was indeed the case for numerous individuals, most religious bodies merely saw it as evidence that God approved their doctrine and structure, and there was little or no change in the old wineskins. However, greater measures of grace are coming and multitudes in the institutional churches will be set on fire to gather in God's gigantic end-time harvest.

(5) The Gospel of the Kingdom Expresses the Heart of God

The fact that one might speak the same words that Jesus used under similar circumstances does not necessarily mean that he is preaching the gospel of the Kingdom. The words of Jesus came from a heart moved by love and compassion for the state of lost men. He wept over the needs of His people. The gospel is not simply a matter of correct words and doctrine, but words and acts rooted in mercy and compassion. Love is a language that the deaf can hear and the blind can see. Those to whom the gospel is preached can sense what is rooted in the spirit and motive of a minister. There must be an empathy in both the heart of the messenger and his message that expresses the heart of God. This is why prayer is so essential; only God can touch us so that we will experience His love and burden for the lost.

A human motive for evangelism is to gain decisions for Christ; a divine unction, on the other hand, will seek out the most unlovely in society, those in the deepest depths of sin, poverty and oppression. To win such as these to Christ reveals the glory and power of God. Numbers are not the goal. It is the poor and helpless in the world who are richer in faith and more likely to come to Him. This is where the gospel of the Kingdom is to focus (Luke 6:20).

This fact is seen by the manner in which Jesus verified His ministry to John the Baptist when John was in prison.

*—Go and report to John what you **hear** and **see**; the **blind** receive sight and the **lame** walk, the **lepers** are cleansed and the **deaf** hear, and the **dead** are raised up, and the **poor** have the gospel preached to them.*

Matthew 11:4-5

The gospel of the Kingdom is **socially relevant!** Because this has not always been true of gospels presented over the centuries, much of what should be the responsibility of the Church today in caring for the poor and afflicted has been taken over by secular governments.

We must ask ourselves how we can preach the gospel of the Kingdom if our hearts are not broken with compassion for the awesome needs of those in the streets of sin, for example, children of the homeless, especially those of drug addicted mothers. Not only must our minds be prepared to preach, but our hearts must also be changed to reveal the mercy of God. Mercy expresses the magnificent dimensions of His love, supply and condescension to meet the needs of sinful men who are incapable of helping themselves. Mercy is a vital ingredient in the gospel of the Kingdom, for without it the good news would never be taken to regions of great poverty or persecution, privation, ignorance or demonic influence. Mercy is seen both in the message of the cross and in those who lay down their lives to take the gospel.

The harvest to be gathered in will require great mercy and compassion, for much of this harvest is destined to come from those in great need (Luke 14:16-24).

*—Go out at once into the streets and lanes of the city and bring in here **the poor and crippled and blind and lame**.*

Luke 14:21b

The question arises: "How can I become more merciful?" The only place to find mercy is at the throne of grace where it is dispensed (Hebrews 4:16). This may require many trips and much time in His presence. One thing that will take place there is that we will develop a greater appreciation of the grace of God in our own lives. However, we must also begin to show mercy and kindness to those around us who are in need. As we do so, our hearts will start to change.

Jesus did not work miracles of healing and deliverance simply to prove who He was. He was moved with compassion and acted out of mercy and love for the afflicted (Matthew 9:36, 14:14, 15:32, 20:30-34). And so must those who minister the gospel of His Kingdom.

It is those who go forth with weeping, sowing the gospel in tears, who will reap souls with joy (Psalm 126:5-6).

(6) The Gospel of the Kingdom Demonstrates the Power of God

—the kingdom of God does not consist in words,
but in power.

First Corinthians 4:20

Jesus did not come to earth just to give us His words; He came to give us Himself. Christ in us, through the Holy Spirit, is our credential and power to preach Him to the world. Thus, to minister the gospel is to minister the Lord of the Word as well as the word of the Lord. It is Jesus who is to be seen and heard! The gospel is God speaking to mankind in His Son (Hebrews 1:1-2). Old Testament prophets spoke for God, but the Son Himself must be **seen and heard** through our gospel. He, not words about Him, is the power of God.

First, the message of the **cross of Christ** is the power of God **for salvation** to everyone who truly repents and believes.

Second, the Holy Spirit attests to the authority of Jesus over sickness and satanic oppression by working signs and wonders through the preaching of the gospel. As Paul testified:

*—in the power of **signs and wonders,** in the power of the Spirit; so that from Jerusalem and round as far as Illyricum **I have fully preached the gospel of Christ.***

Romans 15:18-19

The same demonstration of power was present for other ministries preaching the gospel of the Kingdom in the early Church.

*But Peter said, "I do not possess silver and gold, but **what I do have I give to you.** In the name of Jesus Christ the Nazarene — walk!" And seizing him by the right hand, he raised him up; and immediately his feet and his ankles were strengthened. And with a leap he stood upright and began to walk—.*

Acts 3:6-8

*And Stephen, full of grace and **power,** was performing great wonders and signs among the people.*

Acts 6:8

And Philip went down to the city of Samaria and began proclaiming Christ to them. And the multitudes with one accord were giving attention to what was said by Philip, as they heard and saw the signs which he was performing. For in the case of many who had unclean spirits, they were coming out of them shouting

*with a loud voice; and many who had been
paralyzed and lame were healed.*

Acts 8:5-7

The same signs and wonders are to follow the gospel
of the Kingdom today. Our heart, vision, and commitment must be rooted in faith that the power of Christ
will be seen in the gospel we preach (1 Corinthians 2:5,
Ephesians 6:12, Mark 16:17). Another reason for
desiring signs and wonders is that they might provoke
Israel to jealousy and so turn Jews to faith in their
Messiah.

How can this be done? First, consider the commission given to Adam to cultivate and care for the gar-
den, to name all the creatures and to rule over them.
Second, consider the commission given by Jesus to
His disciples: "—preach, saying, 'The kingdom of
heaven is at hand.' Heal the sick, raise the dead,
cleanse the lepers, cast out demons; freely you
received, freely give" (Matthew 10:7-8).

In both instances, these commissions could only be
carried out from a **position of rest.** Adam had nothing to do with creating the animal and plant life he
ruled over and was responsible for. He had never
studied animal and plant husbandry. The disciples
had no ability within themselves to perform the
spiritual miracles they were asked to do. God was
responsible for all natural life in the first instance,
and for all spiritual life in the second. In both cases,
they were required to have **faith** and be obedient,
trustfully resting in God to do the work. We also are
to minister out of a position of faith and rest (Hebrews
4:10). There is no other way.

We do need to be baptized in the Holy Spirit, but
without purity and humility, the grace and power of
the Holy Spirit will not abide in us; and without faith
and being at rest in Him, grace and power will not be

released through us to those in need. The gospel of the Kingdom is not a message of passive innocence, but of active, militant, dynamic righteousness! We are called to take back that which has been usurped from God's people by the enemy.

Spiritual warfare is a conflict between two kingdoms. Demons hate and react in various ways against the gospel. Our commission is to worship the Lord, resist satan, bind and wrestle in prayer against spiritual authorities, and cast out demons. The days ahead will see great power in lying signs and wonders by satan in the New Age Movement. Through the deception of witchcraft and sorcery, he will seek to turn men away from the government of God and to control them by manipulation, intimidation and domination. The Church is going to be tested by many false ministries with supernatural signs whose goal is to turn people away from the Lord and His gospel. The goal of New Age philosophy is an enlightened mind, whereas the goal of Christianity is a regenerated heart. Because it was the mind of Eve that was involved in her temptation and fall, it is vital, once we are saved, that we seek a renewing of our minds. The battleground in warfare is the mind; this is where one must first win the battle (2 Corinthians 10:3-5, Romans 12:1-2).

(7) The Gospel of the Kingdom Establishes the Government of God

The authority that Jesus possesses as Head over the Church and as Lord of lords was given to Him because He was willing and obedient to lay down His life at Calvary. The cross became the basis of His authority (Philippians 2:5-11). He has been given authority to abolish all other rule, power and dominion so that He alone rules in the Kingdom represented by the earth and its heavens. When this takes place, it will then become part of His Father's Kingdom (1 Corinthians 15:24-28). He is now sitting at the right hand of His Father. From here, He will rule until **all** enemies are under His feet. The task of bringing these enemies into subjection is a work He will do through the Church. And this task begins with us, for His foes are all who are enemies of His cross, including those who profess His Name (Philippians 3:17-18). We must come to the place where we are totally under His government and He has first place in **all areas of our lives** before He will use us to restore His rightful place in the earth and heavens. The government of God is not simply one of external commandments, but of an inner relationship between a loving Father and obedient sons.

He is also Head of the body, the church, — so that He Himself might come to have first place in everything.

Colossians 1:18

Some ministers have made merchandise of the gospel; there have been dishonest and impure motives behind a few who preach it. However, this will cease. God will **never** compromise His holiness or character for the sake of ministry. He will no longer tolerate hypocrisy or hidden sin in the Church, nor will He allow men to control what the Spirit is doing or to build personal kingdoms for their ministry. He is committed to destroying the pride of man, hidden idols and works of the flesh in His Church. He will establish His government in the Church **first of all,** and then He will work through her to bring down and destroy the dominions of darkness.

What do these things mean to us? First of all, we now have authority over **all** of the power of satan and his hosts. Greater is He who is in us than he who is in the world. As believers, we are **never** to be subject in any way to satan. Second, we also have authority to proclaim the gospel, to win men to Christ, to disciple them and to extend the Kingdom of God.

It is in a third area where the Lord's authority and government in His Church is lacking. The Kingdom of God is not made up of individual believers living isolated, independent lives under the Lordship of Christ. The heart of Jesus is to bring His body forth as **one new mighty man of the Spirit** of which He is the Head; a body in which all members are knit together in unity to move as one man. His government is expressed by the obedient response of each individual member to the Head and also by how they submit and relate to one another. His Kingdom is not represented by individuals who do their own thing independently of the rest of His body; it is members loving, forgiving, helping, honoring and submitting to one another in an environment of love, encouragement, trust and fellowship that link them together in a united expression of His government. This is what the Lord will bring forth in the days ahead, both within and between local churches.

Those who preach the gospel of the Kingdom must **not** be satisfied to see converts simply baptized in water and in the Spirit. They are to see them integrated into the life of a local church where they can be equipped for their place of service under the Lordship of Christ. The gospel is not only to bring us out of darkness, but to see us fully **established** under the government of Christ. This is not brought about through the heavy-handed authority of leaders, but by the gentle authority of servanthood that promotes the Lordship of Christ. A biblical eldership will never work where men seek to control what God is doing.

Elders must be men who bend their knees and cultivate their hearts in humility, men who learn to serve, admonish, appreciate and affirm one another in the love of Christ. This establishes the centrality of Jesus and His government.

Paul saw himself, not only as a preacher of the gospel of the Kingdom, but also as a bond-servant serving those who responded to the gospel until they were properly established in a local church. Paul's personal life, as well as his ministry, exemplified the message of the cross. He laid his life down for the sake of the gospel and for those who believed (1 Thessalonians 1:5, 2:4-13).

> *For we do not preach ourselves but Christ Jesus as Lord, and **ourselves as your bond-servants for Jesus' sake.***
>
> Second Corinthians 4:5

Thus, evangelism should be an **accountable** outreach of a local church, where the gospel message will not be hindered by a lack in character or vision of the one bringing the message. An evangelist's commitment must be both to the lost and to the local church. The Lord would not harvest His grain without first building barns to put it in. And the barn of safety, nurture, service and government in a corporate sense is the local church.

As the Church is restored and the gospel of the Kingdom proclaimed, the government of God among His people will become visible to leaders of cities and nations of the world. The glory of God will be seen upon the Church (Isaiah 60:1-5). The strongholds of evil will be brought down from the heavens, and the Kingdom of God will be established in the Church. It is not a time to sit in spiritual armories polishing our weapons; the Church is to rise up, united and militant, and take the gospel out to the afflicted of the world.

If a local church has been unable to equip its saints for service today, bringing them into the maturity which belongs to the fullness of Christ, how can it ever minister to the multitudes of drug afflicted, crippled and oppressed converts that will be coming from the streets of sin in the days ahead? A mighty work of the Holy Spirit is needed to develop scripturally sound local bodies of believers in which **each** member is equipped for service, and in which **all ministries and gifts** of the Spirit are present. The Lord's house is to be a great armory, but it must also be a spiritual hospital for the afflicted and weak. The key for this to take place is to see the government of Christ restored to **all** lives and ministries of the church, to see accountable relationships established, to develop leaders with hearts of bond-servants, and to see **every** member equipped to serve. Finally, it must be clear that the Kingdom of God has to be established in the Church before it can be established in the earth.

(8) Worship is an Essential Mark of the Gospel of the Kingdom

Every individual who has bent his knees in repentance to receive forgiveness of sins can testify of the joy that became his: first, the great relief and gladness that arose from realizing that his sins were buried forever in the sea of God's forgetfulness, never to be remembered again; then the wonder and worship of Jesus whose love had led Him to death on the cross. This aspect of worship will always grow, for to know Him better is to love Him more.

All of this has been true wherever the gospel has been proclaimed over the centuries. It has always brought joy and gladness to those who receive its message and sorrow and darkness to those who reject it.

However, there is a greater dimension in the response of joy that is to be manifested as this age comes to a close. When the prophet Isaiah described the gospel of the Kingdom that Jesus would preach, both at His first advent (Isaiah 61:1-2), and later through His body at the close of this age, it was his reference to the latter that contained these words:

> —*to comfort all who mourn, to grant those who mourn in Zion, giving them a **garland** instead of ashes, the **oil of gladness** instead of mourning, the **mantle of praise** instead of a spirit of fainting.*

Isaiah 61:2c-3

There will be something uniquely different in men's response to the gospel in the days ahead. It is not a matter of being saved; after all, if one is saved, this can't be improved upon. In essence, the difference we can expect to see will be based on three things:

- The depths of deception and lawlessness will exceed in their influence anything previously experienced on earth (Matthew 24:9-24). Those who are converted will have great appreciation of the depths from which they have been delivered.

- Decisions for Christ will be more difficult to make, for there shall exist great persecution of the righteous. It will be evident that there can be no third option; one must be committed to either Christ or the antichrist (2 Thessalonians 2:9-12, Revelation 13:7-8). Converts will make a full, complete surrender to Christ in their conversion or they will not be able to stand. Everyone will be forced to make a decision, either for eternal life or for eternal judgment.

- There will be times of tremendous spiritual warfare for the souls of men between the Lord's army and the forces of darkness. A key to the strength of the Lord's army will be the spiritual songs, the praises and worship of minstrels who lead the Lord's people into battle. Great miracles will take place during these times when the high praises of God resound. The place of rest in spiritual warfare will be found in worship, praise and thanksgiving, for the battle is the Lord's. We enter into His victory. Worship is the universal language of spiritual warfare! The oil of gladness and mantle of praise spoken of by Isaiah will arise from the hearts of those who recognize the great depths of darkness and destruction from which they have been delivered. It will be heard in songs of the Lord given by the Spirit. These songs will be new, songs never before heard on earth. God will do a new thing in revealing His glory as He chooses young people from the deepest pits of sin and transforms them into minstrels to sing the song of the Lord. Glory and worship will be the mantle of His army. There is good worship and praise today, but it is only a taste of what is to come. Two ultimate objectives of the gospel of the Kingdom are to see Jesus come to have first place in everything as King in His Kingdom, and to see His people become a Kingdom of priests who serve Him in worship and intercession.

(9) The Gospel of the Kingdom is a Message of Prophetic Insight

A gospel that does not bring revelation of God's purpose for each day would be incomplete. The gospel of the Kingdom preached by Jesus was centered in the fulfillment of Old Testament prophecies. His message and deeds revealed the purpose and blessing of God for His covenant people, Israel. His advent was God's day of visitation to them. His coming was prepared and announced by John the Baptist, who had a spirit like that of Elijah. John's message, "Repent, for the kingdom of heaven is at hand," was a word of prophetic insight. Jesus came unto His own, for it was God's year of favor to Israel. Isaiah the prophet foretold that Jesus was to —

*—to proclaim the **favorable year of the Lord**—.*
Isaiah 61:2a

Today, as the Lord once more ministers the gospel of the Kingdom, He again has a strategy to bless His covenant people. He plans to raise up His body as a mighty, united army and bring all enemies under His feet through a time of spiritual warfare and evangelism, after which He will return to judge the world. During this time of testing and conflict His bride will be prepared, the tares will be gathered out from the wheat, a great harvest will be gathered in, satan will be vanquished and the purpose of God for this age will be established.

The Lord's strategy to bless the Church is by using her to accomplish His purpose. What He does will be manifested through His people to the principalities above.

—to bring to light what is the administration of the mystery which for ages has been hidden in God, who created all things; in order that the

manifold wisdom of God might now be made known through the church to the rulers and the authorities in the heavenly places. This was in accordance with the eternal purpose which He carried out in Christ Jesus our Lord.

Ephesians 3:9-11

In the history of the Church, there has never been an instance of spiritual fathers bringing forth a succeeding generation of sons who surpassed them in spiritual excellence of character and ministry. As men of God have been raised up over the history of the Church to lead the way into restoration of truth, revival broke forth, only to fade away in succeeding generations. One cannot come into truth from a place of error without conflict. History has shown that this is inevitable. Whoever has "defined truth" and placed boundaries around their definition are not open to new truth.

Change is coming! The Lord is bringing forth a new generation of bond-servants to proclaim the gospel of the Kingdom and to lead His people with prophetic insight into His purpose for these days. They will be men like Elijah with hearts and vision to raise up spiritual sons to take up their mantle and excel them in ministry and spiritual stature.

This principle of excellence is at the heart of the Lord's strategy to bless His people and prepare them for the glory of the days ahead. The grace and power of God upon believers at the end of this age, as well as the forces against them, will be greater than in any previous generation. The Church that is being raised up will **not** be like traditional churches we see today. In that day, the saints will be wholly committed to the Lord and move as a disciplined army under His command. The **youth** are destined to play a significant

role in the Lord's army. This is apparent from the
following translations of Psalm 110:1-3.

*The Lord says to my Lord: "Sit at My right
hand, until I make Thine enemies a footstool for
Thy feet." The Lord will stretch forth Thy strong
scepter from Zion, saying, "Rule in the midst of
Thine enemies." Thy people will volunteer freely
[literally, Thy people will be free will offerings]
in the day of Thy power [literally, of Thy army];
in holy array, from the womb of the dawn, Thy
youth are to Thee as the dew.*

Psalm 110:1-3, NAS

*—Your people will offer themselves willingly in
the day of Your power, in the beauty of holiness
and in holy array out of the womb of the morning; to You will spring forth Your young men
who are as the dew.*

Psalm 110:3, AMP

*—Your people will offer themselves freely on the
day You lead your host upon the holy mountains, from the womb of the morning like dew
Your youth will come to You.*

Psalm 110:3, RSV

Restoration of the Church goes hand in hand with
restoration of the gospel of the Kingdom. Both are
necessary in the purpose of God. The Church requires
leaders with prophetic insight to see the need for the
five-fold ministries of Ephesians 4:11 in order to equip
and prepare the army of the Lord.

The Lord's heart is that there not be a fading away
of fathers as strong, young ministries emerge, but
that **both** the young and the old go forth together in
His army. The wisdom and experience of age are to be
combined with the zeal and strength of youth! Just as
Caleb and Joshua went into the Promised Land

together, so fathers are to join hands and hearts with the youth and go forth together with them. This is the strategy that makes the era ahead become the favorable year of the Lord for His people! It is a key to the victory that lies ahead.

Isaiah spoke of additional prophetic insight in the gospel of the Kingdom that is pertinent to these last days.

To proclaim the day of vengeance of our God—.
Isaiah 61:2b

Satan has a counter-strategy of evil by which he seeks to frustrate the purpose of God and bring in his own new world order. Central in his strategy is the New Age Movement; in concert with its deception, satan has targeted the youth of this generation for destruction, just as he sought to do when Moses and Jesus were born. He is also attempting to destroy godly leadership in homes and churches through the spirit of Jezebel, the dominant evil authority he has placed over this land. A major and important thrust in spiritual warfare facing the Church today is to discern and cast out this manipulating spirit of Jezebel from the lives of individuals, families and churches.

All people will be brought to a place of choosing between good and evil, for there will be two gods: the true God and the god of this world (Christ or the antichrist). There will be two seeds: the seed of the woman and the seed of the serpent (Genesis 3:5); two women: the bride of Christ and the whore; two cities: the New Jerusalem and Babylon; two harvests: the souls of the redeemed and the tares; two options: a regenerated heart or an "enlightened" mind; and two destinies: life or death.

In this conflict, God foreknows all that satan will be allowed to do, and He will even use it for His purpose (Proverbs 16:4). He will cause all who refuse to love the truth, that they might be saved, to believe satan's lie and be lost (2 Thessalonians 2:9-12). This is how He will separate the wicked from the righteous.

Again, the kingdom of heaven is like a dragnet cast into the sea, and gathering fish of every kind; and when it was filled, they drew it up on the beach; and they sat down, and gathered the good fish into containers, but the bad they threw away. So it will be at the end of the age; the angels shall come forth, and take out the wicked from among the righteous, and will cast them into the furnace of fire—.

Matthew 13:47-49a

When the purpose of God is completed, He will execute His judgment and wrath upon satan and all who love evil and lawlessness. It will be the day of His vengeance.

The gospel of the Kingdom would be incomplete if it did not reveal the strategy of the evil one we are to overcome, and make known the purpose and plan of God for His Church. Prophetic insight serves as a beacon of light so that the day of the Lord might not overtake us like a thief in the night (1 Thessalonians 5:1-5).

Finally, the field of harvest is the entire world. There is an acceleration of events taking place; God has sovereignly opened doors for the gospel in communist nations, and now apparently He is beginning to open doors to Islamic nations. We need new dimensions of faith for the grace and resources that will be needed to carry the gospel of the Kingdom through these doors.

CHAPTER FOUR

Warfare that Brings the End

Is the Rapture Next?

After I became a Christian, I joined a local church where I was established in the faith by an excellent Bible teacher. One part of his foundational teaching involved study of last day events. His approach to this subject was centered around the precept of a pre-tribulation rapture of the Church.

Three years later, when the Lord called my wife and I into His service, I was impressed by the Holy Spirit to first develop thorough, clear presentations of major doctrines in order to lay good foundations for truth in those I would be teaching. In the course of doing this, I eventually found myself addressing the theology of God's purpose for His Church in the last days. As I studied and restudied the Scriptures, including a number of authors on this subject, I became convinced that the dispensational teaching of a pre-tribulation rapture was not true. It is simply not supported by Scripture.[5,7]

Once I had taken this position, I prayed for understanding on how to formulate an eschatology that clearly expressed what I believed the Holy Spirit is saying in Scripture concerning the Lord's plan for the Church in the last days. It was in the course of this pursuit that I found myself wrestling for a clearer understanding of Second Thessalonians 2:1-12, particularly, verses 6 and 7.

The Incarnation of satan

As we consider the following Scriptures, it is important to remember that four things play a role when translators attempt to present truth from difficult passages. Accuracy in translating individual words, the quality of syntax in sentences, how well the context of the overall passage is maintained and, most of all, the spirit of revelation. For whatever reason, it would appear that one or more of these factors are weaker in some translations of Second Thessalonians 2:6-7.

In order to avoid an interpretation that would be out of context with the subject being addressed, the text under consideration (2 Thessalonians 2:1-12) will be examined verse by verse.

*Now we request you, brethren, with regard to the **coming of our Lord Jesus Christ, and our gathering together to Him**—.*

Second Thessalonians 2:1

It is perfectly clear that Paul is addressing the second coming of Christ, when believers, alive or dead, are instantly changed, receiving immortal bodies, and then are caught up to meet the Lord Jesus at His return. The following two verses provide additional details of this event.

*Behold, I tell you a mystery; we shall not all sleep, but we shall all be changed, in a moment, in the twinkling of an eye, at the **last** [i.e., seventh] **trumpet;** for the trumpet will sound, and the dead will be raised imperishable, and we shall be changed.*

First Corinthians 15:51-52

*For the Lord Himself will descend from heaven with a shout, with the voice of the archangel, and the dead in Christ shall rise first. Then we who are alive and remain [i.e., **survive**] shall be caught up together with them in the clouds to meet the Lord in the air, and thus we shall always be with the Lord.*

First Thessalonians 4:16-17

Paul is emphasizing that the return of Christ is his **primary** concern. He wants the Church to be well informed on all aspects of this truth.

—that you may not be quickly shaken from your composure or be disturbed either by a spirit or a message or a letter as if from us, to the effect that the day of the Lord has come.

Second Thessalonians 2:2

The believers were told emphatically by Paul that this event, referred to in this verse as "the day of the Lord," had not taken place. It was yet future. They were to disregard any teaching, written communication or prophetic utterance that said otherwise. He then went on to point out **two** necessary and unmistakable events that **must** precede the return of Christ.

*Let no one in any way deceive you, for it will not come unless the **apostasy** comes first, and the* *man of lawlessness is revealed, the son of destruction—.*

Second Thessalonians 2:3

The second coming of Christ will not take place until first a great apostasy takes place. The word apostasy is translated from the Greek word *APOSTASIA*, meaning defection or revolt. It is derived from another Greek word meaning "to lead away or to depart from." Thus, a falling away by many from Christendom must come to pass before the second coming of Christ. This could refer to the falling away that took place in the Dark Ages. It could also refer to the deception of many who are on the fringe of Christendom without a deep personal commitment to Christ. This second possibility is substantiated by other Scriptures such as Matthew 24:4-5, 10-13 and First Timothy 4:1. The ground swell of such a falling away is beginning to be seen, as the deception of the New Age Movement is growing in influence in the nations of the West.

A second event, which must also precede the Lord's return, becomes the primary focus of Paul's words in the remainder of the verses we are considering. This event is the revealing or unveiling of the man of sin (or lawlessness; one who is also called the antichrist and the son of destruction or perdition). "Son of perdition" is used only twice in Scripture, once in reference to Judas Iscariot (John 17:12), and here concerning the man of sin. This unveiling of the man of lawlessness becomes the context in the verses that follow.

—who opposes and exalts himself above every so-called god or object of worship, so that he takes his seat in the temple of God, displaying himself as being God.

Second Thessalonians 2:4

The first points Paul makes concerning the future antichrist are that he will be physically visible and that he will be subject to no one, even proclaiming and projecting himself by his actions as literally being God. It is not clear whether the phrase "temple of God" points to a rebuilt temple in Jerusalem, or whether it refers to the New Age heresy that "Everyone is a (temple) of god." One thing is certain: satan indwells this particular person who is worshiped, for he would allow no lesser evil personage to lay claim to being God. Scripture is quite clear that **all** who are not children of God at this time will indeed worship him.

> *And **all** who dwell on the earth will worship him, everyone whose name has not been written from the foundation of the world in the book of life of the Lamb who has been slain.*
>
> Revelation 13:8

Because of his previous instruction to the believers at Thessalonica, they were probably more clear on what he is saying in these verses than many who have since attempted to interpret Paul's words.

> *Do you not remember that while I was still with you, I was telling you these things? And you know what restrains **him** now, so that in his time he may be revealed!*
>
> Second Thessalonians 2:5-6

The word "him" does not apply to one being restrained in the Greek text. Apparently "him" was added after "restrains" by translators to establish what they thought was being communicated; namely, that someone or something was hindering revelation of the man of sin. However, there is nothing in grammar or syntax that requires someone or something to restrain the one to be revealed. They could possibly be the same person. The change from neuter to the masculine in verse 7, when referring to the restraining influence, shows that it is a person.

The following two translations of verse 6 are more accurate.

> *And now you are aware what is detaining, for him to be unveiled in his own era.* (CLNT: The Concordant Literal New Testament, which is based on the Concordant Greek Text compiled by A.E. Knoch.)

> *And now you know the thing holding back, for him to be unveiled in his time.* (IB: The Interlinear Bible, which is based on the Received Greek Text.)

At this point, we do not know who is being restrained or held back. We **do know** that the subject being addressed is an unveiling of the man of sin (who could also be the one doing the restraining).

> *For the mystery of lawlessness is already at work; only he who now restrains will do so until* **he is taken** *out of the* **way**.

> Second Thessalonians 2:7

This was the verse of Scripture which created in me no small amount of uncertainty and confusion, but which ultimately became the place of revelation. As this verse is translated in the New American Standard version of the Bible (NAS), it would appear to support pretribulation rapture teaching (i.e., the Holy Spirit will restrain lawlessness until He is taken out of the world in the rapture of the Church).

However, research of the Greek text suggests that two words have been poorly translated. The word "taken" is translated from the Greek word *GINOMAI* which actually means, "to come into being, to come to be, to happen or to become." It is so translated approximately two hundred times in the NAS. It is translated "taken" in conjunction with the word "out" **only** in this particular verse. The word "way" is translated from the Greek word *MESOS*, which means "middle or in the midst." It is so translated over forty-six times in the NAS. It is only translated as "way," implying reference to space or location, in this one verse. (It is also translated as "way" in Colossians 2:14 where the meaning is "to nullify.")

Whatever the rationale was for translating these words as they appear in the NAS and several other translations, a question arises: Why not assign the preferred English equivalents to these words, and leave interpretation to the Holy Spirit? The following translations apparently did this.

*For the secret of lawlessness is already operating. Only when the present detainer may be **coming** to be **out of the midst**.* (CLNT)

*For the mystery of lawlessness already is working. Only he is holding back now, until it **comes out of the midst**.* (IB)

The phrase "out of the midst" implies that the one restraining will appear out from the midst of people on earth, suggesting that his restraining influence will cease or change at that point in time.

And then that lawless one will be revealed whom the Lord will slay with the breath of His mouth and bring to an end by the appearance of His coming.

Second Thessalonians 2:8

Let's review Paul's message from verse six through verse eight. There exists a present restraining influence of believers by the mystery of lawlessness, a

satanic influence that will continue until, at some
time in the future, there will occur a worldwide appearance of this evil man of sin. His visible coming to
earth is spoken of as an unveiling which apparently
will involve his physical, visible presence. We know
from other Scriptures that this man is the antichrist,
the number of whose name is 666. We can now conclude that Paul is speaking about the restraining
influence of this man of sin **upon the lives and
ministries of the saints.**

The following is a possible paraphrase of the
teaching that Paul may have previously given to
the believers at Thessalonica: "Do not let anyone
deceive you into believing that the day of the Lord
has already come. It will not take place until, **first,**
through deception satan will cause many to turn
away from the Christian faith. Beware of his deception. **Second,** before the Lord Jesus returns, there
will also be a physical appearance of this man of
lawlessness in the earth. He is to be unveiled before
all mankind. Today satan is the 'accuser of the
brethren.' He restrains you through evil oppres-
sions of condemnation, accusation, intimidation
and manipulation. He is at war against the Church
and the angels of God. He also restrains you
through the influence of evil angelic authorities in
the heavens who direct demons upon the earth. At
the present time he is prince of the authority of the
air over those forces who are against the Lord and
His Church. He will continue to accuse, condemn
and oppress the saints until such time as he is
displaced from heaven and is unveiled on earth,
making his appearance as the dominant authority
figure of all evil. He will continue to persecute the
Church, but he will no longer be a restrainer in
heaven between us and the Lord."

It was at this point of discovery that the Lord revealed to me the relationship between Revelation 12 and these verses in Thessalonians.

*And there was war in heaven, Michael and his angels waging war with the dragon. And the dragon and his angels waged war, and they were not strong enough, and there was **no longer a place found for them in heaven.** And the great dragon was thrown down, the serpent of old who is called the devil and satan, who deceives the whole world; **he was thrown down to the earth, and his angels were thrown down with him.** And I heard a loud voice in heaven, saying, "**now the salvation, and the power, and the kingdom of our God and the authority of His Christ have come, for the accuser of our brethren has been thrown down,** who accuses them before our God day and night. And **they overcame him** because of the blood of the Lamb and because of the word of their testimony, and they did not love their life even to death. For this reason, rejoice, O heavens and you who dwell in them. Woe to the earth and the sea, because the devil has come down to you, having great wrath, knowing that he has only a short time."*

Revelation 12:7-12

*Now at that time Michael, the great prince who stands guard over the sons of your people, will arise. And there **will be a time of distress such as never occurred since there was a nation** until that time; and at that time your people, everyone who is found written in the book, will be rescued.*

Daniel 12:1

It is clear that the unveiling of the man of sin takes place after a period of spiritual warfare which sees satan thrown out of heaven along with his angels. This is in accordance with the Lord's purpose for the last days. There will be a militant, overcoming spirit of power and authority resting upon the Church as she prepares for her Lord's return. This will come to fullness when satan is cast out of heaven, for then there will no longer be any evil influence in the heavens between the Church and her Lord. It will be a time of great salvation, power and authority in the Church. The heavens will be open! The glory of God will rest upon her, and there will be a final great harvest of souls into the Kingdom (Isaiah 60:1-5, Luke 14:16-23). The increased power and authority resting upon the saints will be directly related to the open heavens, from which satan and his authorities will have been cast out. In these days there will be an increased, and probably more visible, ministry of angels helping the Church.

At this time satan, having lost his place of authority in heaven, will take up the place of ultimate authority and power over all religion in the earth. He will do this by becoming incarnate in a man, one who will be recognized by Christians as the antichrist. Thus there will arise great persecution of righteousness in the earth, for the antichrist will require all peoples to worship him. More than anything else, satan seeks to be worshiped. Knowing that man will not generally worship what he cannot see, satan will become visible through incarnation. It is this unveiling of satan as the man of lawlessness that will point to the imminent return of the Lord in glory. The day of the Lord will not come until this unveiling takes place.

The climax of incarnation in satan's strategy of evil may be intended as his imitation of the incarnation of

Jesus. It is even possible that this incarnation will be an attempt by satan to imitate the Lord's resurrection by using a dead body to which he gives life at his incarnation.

> *And I saw one of his heads as if it had been **slain** [literally, as having been slain to death, IB], and his **fatal wound was healed.** And the whole earth was amazed and followed after the beast; and they worshiped the dragon [satan] because he gave his authority to the beast; and they worshiped the beast, saying, "Who is like the beast, and who is able to wage war with him?"*

> Revelation 13:3-4

At the time of his appearance, satan's long range strategy, centered in the New Age Movement, will have culminated in the deception of many thousands of individuals through false supernatural signs and wonders. The persecution of Christians will see many lay down their lives in martyrdom. However, whether in death or life, **they will overcome him because great power and grace will rest upon the Church!**

The remaining four verses of the passage of Scripture being studied provide further insight into this future period of time.

> *—that is, the one whose coming is in accord with the activity of satan, with all power and signs and false wonders, with all the deception of wickedness for those who perish, because they did not receive the love of the truth so as to be saved. And for this reason **God will send upon them a deluding influence** so that they might believe what is false, in order that they all may*

be judged who did not believe the truth, but took pleasure in wickedness.

Second Thessalonians 2:9-12

These are days when the seal which God placed on the vision given to Daniel is being removed, and revelation is beginning to open up the meaning of events that will take place in the last days (Daniel 12:4, 8-9).

Before the Lord returns, there will be a separation of the wicked from the righteous. There will also be a purging and refining of His people during the days of antichrist; the bride will make herself ready. It is tribulation before rapture, endurance before reigning, testing before glory and, for some, martyrdom before a crown.

*But immediately **after the tribulation of these days**—the sign of the Son of Man will appear in the sky—and they will see the Son of Man coming on the clouds of the sky with power and great glory. And He will send forth His angels with a great trumpet and they will gather together His elect from the four winds—.*

Matthew 24:29-31

*After these things I looked, and behold, a **great multitude,** which no one could count, from every nation and all tribes and peoples and tongues, standing before the throne and before the Lamb—These are the ones who come **out of the great tribulation,** and they have washed their robes and made them white in the blood of the Lamb.*

Revelation 7:9a, 14b

The time ahead is **not** one to fear, for the Lord will never leave nor forsake us!

*When you pass through the waters, I will be
with you; and through the rivers, they will not
overflow you. When you walk through the fire,
you will not be scorched, nor will the flame burn
you.*

Isaiah 43:2

To prepare His saints for the days ahead, the Lord
brings us into places and times of testing so that areas
of weakness and character flaws can be surfaced and
dealt with (1 Peter 1:6-7; 2 Corinthians 4:17; Romans
5:1-5, 8:17-18; 1 Peter 2:21-23; James 1:2-4, 12).

*Beloved, do not be surprised at the fiery ordeal
among you, which comes upon you for your
testing, as though some strange thing were happening to you—.*

First Peter 4:12

If one is unable to embrace trials and tribulations
today, he will not be able to overcome the greater
testings ahead. The cross we find in our circumstances is an expression of the purpose of God for our life.
It is for our good and His glory.

Be Prepared for Tribulation

The early Church was troubled by false teaching
which declared the day of the Lord had already taken
place, and so there was no reason to look forward to
His personal return. Today, much of the Church has
been taught that the Lord will return to rapture the
saints before the great tribulation takes place. However, He is coming for a bride who will be an overcoming people those who have been tested, purified and
found faithful in His service; and she will participate
with Him in His judgment (Jude 14-15).

This is consistent with the understanding given to
Daniel in his vision of the last days.

And some of those who have insight will fall, in order to refine, purge and make them pure, until the end time; because it is still to come at the appointed time.

Daniel 11:35

Many will be purged, purified and refined; but the wicked will act wickedly, and none of the wicked will understand, but those who have insight will understand.

Daniel 12:10

The travail of tribulation **must** come to bring forth an overcoming company from the Church with insight who will walk in the authority and power of Christ to instruct and help other believers. This company of overcomers will minister to the Church, much in the way that Joseph ministered to his family during the great famine that covered the earth in his day. The greatest rewards belong to these overcomers.

And he who overcomes, and he who keeps My deeds until the end, to him I will give authority over the nations.

Revelation 2:26

He who overcomes, I will make him a pillar in the temple of My God, and he will not go out from it anymore; and I will write upon him the name of My God, and the name of the city of My God, the new Jerusalem, which comes down out of heaven from My God, and My new name.

Revelation 3:12

He who overcomes, I will grant to him to sit down with Me on My throne, as I also overcame and sat down with My Father on His throne.

Revelation 3:21

I believe we have already entered the time period called the day of the Lord. I realize this phrase primarily refers to an actual day in which the Lord returns. However, it also includes an indefinite preceding period of time when the Lord judges and prepares His Church, when there is great shaking among the nations and great deception abounds, and when Jews are being gathered back to Israel. We must be able to judge the day in which we live and understand what the Lord is saying for **this hour.** There are no neutral grounds ahead; only great judgment or great blessing. For example, there will certainly be severe judgment on our nation because of the great sins of abortion, drugs, murder, blasphemy and divorce. Indeed, AIDS is undoubtedly a present plague of God's judgment upon the land. We can expect to see a devastating economic collapse in the nineties that will affect the whole earth.

In the realm of the Spirit, there are two opposing strategies: the Lord's strategy for His people and a counter-strategy of satan. There is no question who is going to win; the issue is the role we will play.

If believers are not wholly committed to the Lord and are unfamiliar with these strategies, they face two potential losses:

- Missing an opportunity to participate with the Lord in His great end-time work in and through the Church.

- Being ineffective in spiritual warfare and open to possible deception.

Let us examine an overview of these two strategies.

The Strategy of satan

Satan has a strategy of deception centered in the New Age Movement[8] by which he seeks to frustrate the purpose of God. His ultimate goal is to be worshiped as God by the world. Therefore, while he seeks to capture every soul, he knows that this will not be achieved simply by promoting atheism and unbridled lawlessness alone. For this reason, his primary focus is religious deception. The spirit of Jezebel plays a significant role in this deception.

Satan has placed certain fallen angels as authorities of darkness over populated cities, regions and countries. Operating through demons, these principalities exercise specific roles of wickedness in deception and warfare against mankind. The spirit of Jezebel, one of these spirit beings, is the **dominant** authority of evil over our nation today!

There are several manifestations of this spirit which become apparent from observing the demonic behavior of Queen Jezebel, whom it controlled. The wicked acts of the queen are why this being is called the spirit of Jezebel. Each characteristic represents a unique demonic influence that was present in her life and which continues to mark this spirit today.

- It is a spirit that seeks to control men and women, but primarily women, and to manipulate others through them, often through sexual means. Jezebel fed four hundred prophets of the Asherah (a wooden symbol of a female deity) at her table. Her pagan religion included the practice of fertility rites. Besides having a debasing effect on the practitioner, the acts of worship included male and female cultic prostitutes in hetero- and homosexual liaisons. Such corrupt practices as child sacrifice and licentious worship also marked religious devotion to Baal, whom Jezebel also served.

- It is a controlling, rebellious spirit that resists all law and godly authority, especially male authority. Although Ahab, her husband, was king over Israel, it was really Jezebel who ruled. She, not Ahab, defined and led the retaliation against Elijah (1 Kings 19:2).

- It is a lying, accusing, manipulating spirit. Jezebel manipulated men of authority to have the man Naboth falsely accused and then stoned to death in order to steal a vineyard he owned (1 Kings 21:1-16).

- It is a spirit of devastating fear and discouragement. After Elijah slew the prophets of Baal, demons of fear and discouragement troubled him greatly, so much so that he wanted to die (1 Kings 19:3-4, 10-14).

- It is a spirit of witchcraft and the occult. Jezebel served Baal, supported four hundred and fifty demonic prophets of Baal and was instrumental in leading the nation of Israel into idolatry.

- It is a spirit of murder and hatred of the Word of God. Jezebel destroyed the Lord's prophets in Israel (1 Kings 18:4), and she tried to kill Elijah. She played the role of chief priestess to the Baal of that area (Melkarth), a god that required the burning of innocent children as oblations on his altar.

This spirit, which has been in the world for centuries, has, in the strategy of satan, been placed over this nation in recent years to bring about the same breakdown in morals that it accomplished over Israel in the days of Ahab and Jezebel. A primary focus of satan has been to destroy the family and, in particular, the children. The controlling, dominating spirit of Jezebel is the very antithesis of the meekness and submission which are the qualities of godly women. This spirit seeks to emasculate the headship of man which God has ordained for the family and for leadership in the Church.

The following are examples and consequences of the works of the Jezebel spirit in our nation.

- The high and increasing divorce rate.

- The Feminist Movement.

- The current growth in number of abortions, and the related "Pro-choice" Movement among women.

- The permissive lifestyle philosophy that says, "If it feels right, do it," and the corresponding increase in drug abuse and premarital sex.

- The prominent place of women in the leadership of religious cults (e.g., Christian Science, Unity, Theosophy and Astrology), and as mediums in channeling within the New Age Movement.

- The rapid increase of mind control based on altered states of consciousness of the New Age Movement (e.g., séances, channeling, T.M., yoga and self-actualization techniques such as Silva Mind Control).

- The consequences of extreme fear and discouragement in crippling ministries, physical sickness and suicide.

- The promotion of **all** of the above through the various media, especially television.

The spirit of Jezebel has not only affected our society, but it has also made inroads in churches. One such ancient influence of this spirit in Christendom can be seen in the practice of presenting God to the people as a small baby in the arms of His mother and encouraging prayer to her as a mediatress. A second, more recent, example is use of "Mother" as an acceptable alternative to "Father" when addressing Jehovah God. A third example is the increasing acceptance of women for ordination into the clergy.

Of course, the closer a church walks in the ways of the world, the greater will the previous list of social influences become apparent in it. Ordination of homosexuals is one such example. The only answer to such influences is **total repentance** and **commitment** to the Lord.

It is not only lukewarm or backslidden churches that are affected by this spirit. In fact, it appears to be satan's ploy in his attack on the more spiritual assemblies. This was apparently the case of the church at Thyatira. Consider the Lord's word to this church:

> *I know your **deeds**, and your **love** and **faith** and **service** and **perseverance**, and that your deeds of late are greater than at first.*
>
> Revelation 2:19

After such words of commendation, it would seem almost impossible to imagine anything amiss in such a church! However, the Lord goes on to say:

> *But I have this against you, that you **tolerate** the woman Jezebel, who calls herself a **prophetess**, and she **teaches** and **leads My bond-servants astray**—.*
>
> Revelation 2:20

There is no higher calling for a believer in this life than to be a bond-servant for Christ. Thus, these Scriptures deal with the more spiritual people of a spiritual church. It was the **very best** of the saints who were led astray, not by a woman, but by the

prophetic evil spirit of Jezebel. The goal of its deception, shown in verse 24, was to subtly introduce "the
deep things of satan" to eventually corrupt and mis-
lead the church. This is a remarkably accurate definition of satan's objective in the New Age Movement. It
is not enough to serve the Lord with great zeal; we
must also be men and women of His presence in order
to protect our hearts from error.

The real fault of the Thyatiran church was apparently the tolerance of its leadership to so-called
prophetic messages that were not from God. The
elders failed to discern the spirit behind these "revelations," and they did not judge their contents by the
Word of God. How can believers guard themselves
from the spirit of Jezebel?

The place of victory over this spirit **begins** with
godly character that is rooted in humility and submission. This is, first, a submission to the Lord, and
secondly, a submission to those over us in the Lord. It
is particularly important for wives to honor the headship of their husband and for single sisters to honor
the oversight of their elders. The **primary** assault of
Jezebel is against all godly male authority. This spirit
seeks to manipulate leaders, whether in family oversight or church government. Jezebel hates male
leaders who declare the Word of God with authority
and who give clear direction to the church. I am
considering these things within the context of a
spiritual church environment where husbands do
hear from God through their wives and where elders
do recognize and receive the prophetic words of the
Lord through other members of the body of Christ.

There appears to be no evidence that lack of submission was an issue at Thyatira. Thus, a **second** vital
step in defense is to be equipped by the Holy Spirit and
the Word of God so as to recognize what is false and

opens the door to deception. In essence, this requires gifts of the Holy Spirit (i.e., word of knowledge and discerning of spirits) and clear knowledge from Scriptures as to how the spirit of Jezebel can initiate deception into the minds of even spiritual believers.

The following are some examples of what believers and leadership must guard against. They may come in the form of impressions, revelations, prophetic messages, words from other believers or dreams. **In all cases,** they are to be rejected. To believe or embrace them is to **potentially** become open to the demonic influence of this spirit. This can lead to deception and to introducing that deception into the church.

- "Your husband doesn't understand spiritual things; you are the real spiritual leader of your family."

- "Your spouse doesn't understand you, but that person's spouse does; therefore, confide in him (her)."

- "You have revelations; the elders and the rest of the church do not understand. Therefore, leave the church and go develop your ministry."

- "Sexual relations are carnal; therefore, leave your spouse and children to follow me."

- "Use sex to persuade your husband to allow you to assume the ministry and role of spiritual leadership in your family."

- "Use your service (prayer, talents, giving, spiritual gift) to influence the elders to seek your input for their decisions. You should be recognized for your spirituality."

- "The elders are not spiritual and do not have the mind of God for the church. I have given you revelations and directions for the church to follow."

- "The elders lack spiritual insight and wisdom; they are unable to give you counsel, so just ignore their words."

- Unexpected and overwhelming spirits of fear or discouragement

- Desires for sexual fantasies

Church leaders should also be aware of two other messages of deception:

- "Your church is the most spiritual and the only right one; don't associate with leaders of other churches, for you are my special people."

- "You do not have to be accountable to other men; you alone are leader of the church."

Lack of accountability is a major reason why many leaders fall into sin and their ministry is discredited. The spirit of Jezebel will seek to prevent the accountability of a biblical eldership being established for local church government. Satan wants men of God to be independent and to stand alone. The Lord wants His leaders to be dependent and accountable to their peers, something that cannot be done from a remote location since it involves one's daily life.

There are many other demonic forces of evil and deception making up satan's strategy, and we are not to be ignorant of any of them. However, I have addressed this particular spirit because of the great influence it is having in our nation and churches.

New Age Deception

Although New Age teaching and practice is a demonic, counterfeit gospel, it is highly deceptive to the unsaved. This is because it is based on supernatural manifestations, and because many of its statements appear to correspond in a subtle manner to Christian statements of faith; in fact, they contradict them, but they easily deceive those who do not know the Word of God, especially professional, well-educated persons. The following are some examples:

CHRISTIAN	NEW AGE
The new birth	Reincarnation, rebirth
Led by the Holy Spirit	Led by spirit guides through channeling
The Millennium Age	The Astrological Age of Aquarius
Salvation is in Christ	Salvation is within you
Jesus is God	Yes, but no more than you can be by attaining christ-consciousness
Meditate on the Lord	Do yoga; chant a mantra
A regenerated heart	An enlightened mind
A new creature in Christ	A new awareness of reality by experiencing a paradigm shift
Regeneration	An altered state of consciousness
Grow spiritually	Become self-actualized
Love God	Love yourself
God is personal, and His presence is within us	God is a cosmic energy vibrating everywhere; get in tune with it
Stature is reflected in humility and repentance	Stature is based on self-esteem and self-worth
God's will and Word directs my life	My life is based on self-determination
The Bible is God's revelation of truth	New Age theology is an update to the Bible
There is good and evil	There is no good or evil; they are two sides of the same coin

Mystery Babylon

> *And upon her forehead a name was written,*
> *a mystery, "BABYLON THE GREAT, THE*
> *MOTHER OF HARLOTS AND OF THE*
> *ABOMINATIONS OF THE EARTH."*
>
> Revelation 17:5

Who, or what, is the mystery that Scripture describes as a woman of great evil called Babylon? What role does she play in satan's strategy? One can make the following observations from a study of Babylon in Revelation chapters 17 and 18, along with other related Scriptures.

- The essential essence of Babylon is spiritual. While there are references to cities, mountains and kings, the origin and basic purpose of Babylon is satan's attempt to deceive society on a multinational level through the influence of demons (Revelation 18:2).

- Although the spirit of Babylon has been in existence over the centuries, the ultimate manifestation of her evil and identity will only come to fullness at the end of this age. Over the years Bible scholars have interpreted Scriptures concerning Babylon in various ways (e.g., an Islamic religious expansion associated with the rebuilt city of Babylon, the Roman Catholic church, the U.S.A.). However, as this age draws to a close and satan's strategy of evil unfolds, the identity of Babylon will cease to be a mystery to Christians.

- The unholy, self-centered, sensuous religion of Babylon will deceive mankind from nations all over the earth (Revelation 17:15, 18:3). The reason for such widespread deception lies in the unique liaison she has with the antichrist. Scripture describes the woman as riding a scarlet beast which has seven heads and ten horns. The antichrist is described in Scripture as just such a beast (Revelation 13:1-4, 17:3). Satan is the hidden source of the authority and power with which he, in turn, supports the woman and deceives the people.

- The multinational influence and control antichrist achieves through the great harlot is not merely because of a display of satan's power in lying signs and wonders (2 Thessalonians 2:9, Revelation 13:13), but also because she is an unholy blend of religion, government (Revelation 17:18), commerce (Revelation 13:17, 18:10-19) and the arts (Revelation 18:22). In other words, an integrated demonic influence will exist at authority levels across **all of society.** This represents the new world order that satan seeks to bring to pass. The ultimate goal of New Age philosophy is the establishment of one world government and one world religion.

- At the peak of her power, the mother of harlots views herself as a queen (Revelation 18:7). In reality, she is a counterfeit church, a counterfeit bride, the very antithesis of the bride of Christ. She has prostituted every godly virtue and for that reason is called the mother of harlots. Born-again Christians who are in churches that fall away from the faith and begin to embrace New Age teaching must leave those churches immediately (Revelation 18:4)!

- As the New Age Movement becomes more established in the world, this false religious system will bring great persecution upon true believers (Revelation 13:7, 17:6, 18:24).

The future potential of spiritual Babylon can be seen today, especially in western nations, by the growing acceptance of the New Age message in professional groups. This is true in particular for education, politics, business, psychology, religion and the media. It has also gained support from secular humanists, self-actualization or human potential groups, and holistic medicine. The heart of New Age teaching is to turn people away from the absolute truths of God's Word; we are told that everything is an illusion, and therefore we must ignore our rational, critical mind in order to achieve a new inner consciousness of truth through the guidance of "ascended masters" (who are actually demons). Channeling, séances or any endeavor to seek guidance from those with familiar spirits, spiritists or mediums is an abomination to the Lord (Leviticus 20:6, Deuteronomy 18:9-12, Isaiah 8:19).

It is important to recognize that the New Age Movement is an umbrella of satanic oversight that networks and supports his many diverse expressions of evil, such as the growing Islamic movement, apostate Christianity, witchcraft, channeling, astrology, satanism, yoga, reincarnation, transcendental meditation, mind control therapy, U.F.O. experiences/encounters, spiritualist churches and out of body experiences. The heart of the New Age message promotes the ancient temptation to be like God. "There is no creator God," the New Age says. "You are gods. You make your own creation. There is no sin, no judgment, no hell."

New Age teaching is a counterfeit gospel designed to bring in a new age of peace and enlightenment, the Age of Aquarius. The consequences and judgment of satan's strategy are what we read about in Revelation chapters 17 and 18.

The Lord's Strategy

There is a divine strategy in place by which the Lord will restore and prepare His Church, equip His army for a mighty final conflict of spiritual warfare, and bring into His house a great harvest of souls before He returns to judge the world.

The spirit of Elijah is vital to this strategy. Despite all the truth that has been and is being restored to the Church since the time of Martin Luther, there is one significant deficiency yet to be addressed. I do not say restored, for it was also missing in the early Church. There has never been a generation of spiritual fathers who brought forth a generation of sons (converts) that surpassed them in excellence of character and ministry. Historically, when some truth was restored to the Church through a great man of God, his followers built a denominational monument to that truth and resisted further light. Restored truth would then arise through another man in later generations, but always with the same result. Thus, truth has been exploited by leaders to divide the body of Christ rather than bringing it into unity of the faith. A change is coming! The Church the Lord will return for will be united in Him, fully manifesting His character, power and authority and demonstrating the fulfillment of Scriptures such as Ephesians 4:11-16, John 17:20-23, Acts 3:17-21 and Joel 2:23-25. This great work in the Church concerns the spirit of Elijah. His spirit, which was like that of John the Baptist, was an **essential** requirement for the Lord's first advent. The spirit of Elijah is equally necessary to prepare the Church for His second coming.

Behold, I am going to send you Elijah the prophet before the coming of the great and terrible day of the Lord. And he will restore the

*hearts of the fathers to the children, and the
hearts of the children to their fathers, lest I
come and smite the land with a curse.*

Malachi 4:5-6

*And His disciples asked Him, saying, "Why
then do the scribes say that Elijah must come
first?" And He answered and said, "Elijah is
coming and will restore all things; but I say to
you, that Elijah already came, and they did not
recognize him, but did to him whatever they
wished—."*

Matthew 17:10-12

Just as the Lord has recently removed the leaders
of many communist nations to open doors for the
gospel, so also will He raise up in Christendom a new
generation of bond-servants to lead and prepare His
Church. They will be men like Elijah. They will have
hearts and a vision to raise up spiritual sons that
excel them in ministry and, eventually, in stature.
They will not seek to build a kingdom around their
person and ministry, for they will have the spirit of
Elijah resting upon them.

The greatest miracle ever accomplished by Elijah
took place during the years when he imparted to
Elisha what God had built into him. It created a godly
desire in Elisha to receive the anointing that rested on
Elijah, along with understanding of how to avoid the
weaknesses of character Elijah displayed in his conflict with Jezebel (i.e., fear, discouragement, self-pity).
The fruit of this miracle was evident when Elisha
performed similar miracles—but twice as many as
Elijah, without any Scripture record of fear and discouragement.

The traditional mindset of many ministers today
is to pass on authority at death to someone on staff to

carry on their ministry. This is unscriptural and contrary to developing spiritual excellence. One can pass nothing on at death; it must be imparted while we are alive! The story of Elijah and Elisha illustrates this principle of truth.

The final victory over Jezebel did not occur in the days of Elijah. It took place during the lifetime of Elisha when Jehu was king over Israel. In the final spiritual conflict of this age, a vital part of the Lord's army will be young warriors who have been trained by godly fathers with the spirit of Elijah. This is a fundamental principle of excellence in the Lord's end-time strategy for His Church. The second conflict between Elijah and Jezebel is about to begin! The Lord is apprehending a new generation of bond-servant leaders with hearts to raise up overcomers from the youth and older saints, to build the army of the Lord and to prepare the Church for His return. The spirit of Elijah will rest upon them to bring forth these end-time Elishas. Because they have the current word of the Lord for His Church, just as Elijah did for Israel in his day, these men of God are going to be attacked by the Jezebel spirit. God will allow this in order to test and teach His children to overcome. Thus, the more spiritual saints can expect the assault of this spirit, for it will be part of the training, purging and refining process that prepares them for victory. The examples of deceptive overtures already presented show clearly the type of subtle errors satan uses to gain an opening in spiritual believers so as to divide believer from believer, husband from wife, believers from the eldership, leader from leader and church from church. All sin can follow once God's authority is manipulated or destroyed in group relationships.

The spirit of Jezebel had the last word in her conflict with Elijah. But the Elijahs of today are **not** to run in fear or be discouraged. This is a day of victory!

Children Today, Warriors Tomorrow

How does one prepare the youth in the local church to become warriors in the Lord's army? What is required over and beyond the normal training of Christian children? First of all, who should be trained? The twenty to thirty-year-olds at the end of the 90's are the ten to twenty-year-olds today; teenagers at that time are three to nine-year-olds today. Since we don't know the year of His return, children of all ages are candidates. And such training must necessarily include the parents!

Because of the Lord's great grace in the coming days of harvest, there will be some young people saved whom the Lord will sovereignly bring forth quickly into His service, much as He called Jeremiah to be a prophet (Jeremiah 1:6-10). However, this will not be the norm; parents and church leaders are responsible to equip and prepare their youth for the time of darkness ahead. The place of fathers and mothers in training youth is central in Scripture. In spite of all the training found in youth meetings, a proper foundation in character should include the godly input of Christian parents and families. Children who honor and obey their parents are promised a long and good life. Satan is attacking the family in **every** possible way. He is dividing parents from their children. Youth workers must not be a substitute parent for those who do have Christian parents; rather, they must seek and pray for the spirit of Elijah to join the hearts of fathers to the children.

Clearly, fathers must do more than verbally instruct their children. It has been said that one who only hears truth will forget it; one who sees truth in action will remember it; but one who obeys truth understands and possesses it. Thus, fathers in the church are to teach the young, while being an example of what they teach and participating with them in ministry (Proverbs 20:7).

It should not be necessary to amplify the need to intercede for our young people, a burden that begins with the birth of each child. One who grows up seeing the fruit of prayers for him by parents and others will recognize that intercessory prayer is indispensable in spiritual warfare.

Traditional oversight of youth in churches has tended to focus on preparing them to walk in righteousness as adults, while insulating and protecting them from warfare with the forces of evil. Because of the vicious and rapidly growing onslaught of the enemy against children, this must change. There is not one set of spiritual gifts for adults and another set for children. The Holy Spirit can reveal the Lord and expose the evil one to the hearts of children just as He does for adults.

It is unfortunate that many Christians never fully understand the reality of demons and their arenas of influence until adulthood, and often only then through unfortunate experiences. It is **vital** that today's young people be prepared to stand against the deceptions of satan, for it is they whom he has targeted for destruction, just as he attempted to thwart the purpose of God in Moses and Jesus by destroying multitudes of children. His assault on the unsaved youth today is devastating, widespread and growing at an alarming rate. Satan's tools of deception include music (metallic hard rock and subliminal recorded messages), drugs, the occult, fantasy role-playing games, witchcraft and even satanism.

Another important truth to be taught is that wherever there are idols, there will be demons. When one brings an idol into his life, that person opens a door for demonic activity. In this country, the issue is not idols of stone or wood, nor is it idols associated with living creatures (such as snakes or cows as in Hinduism). The issue in our land of affluence is **greed and covetousness** (Colossians 3:5, Ephesians 5:5).

It is not only material things one may covet; it can also be carnal desire for a place of ministry or a position in the church. Any doctrinal emphasis, organization, ministry or minister that occupies a place of esteem and influence in someone's life above that of the Lord Jesus is an idol to that person. And wherever there is an idol, there will be demonic influence!

Oversight for youth meetings should be sensitive to how the Holy Spirit would move rather than following a fixed format. Where possible, and when appropriate, leadership input should come from the more mature of the youth. As the older youth respond to the Lord they become role models for the younger ones to emulate.

Young people should not be viewed as second class members of the church, but should be honored as a specific and important part of the body of Christ. It is often little things that show honor, for example, referring to them as "young adults" rather than "teenagers." Another example would be to provide resources for seminars and retreats with youth from other assemblies.

The transition to participating in body ministry with adults in the central meetings is often difficult for young believers. This is made easier when they are also active in a home church as well as youth meetings.

Because the crowd is smaller and the format more informal, the atmosphere in home meetings is less likely to make younger members self-conscious.

Honest and clear instruction on what lies ahead for the church should be part of youth training, so that young believers can intelligently commit themselves wholeheartedly to the Lord and His purpose for their lives. They must understand that theirs is a generation of decision, before whom God has drawn a line in the sand called **love of truth**; every person must choose to be on one side or the other. Those who will love the truth and serve the Lord should be taught how deeply He loves them and that He will **never leave nor forsake them.** They are His precious treasures.

They must be taught and prepared to walk in a society destined to become one of the most ungodly in mankind's history. It is for this same society that they will be equipped with the mercy and grace of God to evangelize, loving and caring for those who turn to the Lord. They will be part of those workers hired and sent into His vineyard at the eleventh hour.

What lies ahead in persecutions, challenges and world conditions, as well as grace for ministry, will not be like circumstances in the lives of their fathers. All will be new; the future will **not** be like the past!

The professional and spectator roles of clergy and laity will fade away. The body of Christ is being raised up as a mighty man in the earth, as an army through which the Lord can move. The local church will become the Lord's seminary, as was the early Church. Here the saints will be equipped for service and ministries raised up. This involves more than learning theology; it is an "on the job" syllabus of developing godly character, relational integrity, accountability, and learning to minister under the anointing of the

Holy Spirit. While there may be some locations prepared for spiritual training, youth should **not** plan to attend Bible schools or seminaries. This period of time in their lives should be spent on secular training so that they are equipped to support themselves, as necessary, in their service for Christ. To support one's self by secular work as a minister of the Lord is not a lack of faith; on the contrary, it is an act of faith.

Finally, parents ought to teach their children in early childhood that an angel of the Lord is always near to protect them. Once they have this knowledge, the Lord will often open their eyes to see the angel. This reinforces their faith in the Lord's care for them, and it also prepares them for the possible ministry of angels in their later years of serving the Lord. Each major historical period of God's dealings with His people is marked by the ministry of angels. I expect the closing years of this age of grace to experience the greatest manifestation of angelic ministry ever seen as the Lord works through His armies in heaven and on earth (Hebrews 1:3-4; Revelation 8:2, 12:7-9, 19:14).

The Power of Unity

The Lord will work in a mighty way in the days ahead to restore unity of Spirit and faith throughout His body. This unity is vital to the success of His army, and it must begin with leaders. Racism **must be** purged from the Church through deep repentance and reconciliation.

The day is over when we can allow petty human issues to separate us from working with other bodies of believers in the fields of harvest. I doubt if we truly realize how important our unity is in the eyes of the Lord. The anointing that the Lord will send upon His body in the days ahead will bring to pass a great demonstration of unity. This will be one of the most important of the last days miracles.

It is a great blessing to see men of God arising today with a burden to bring leaders of churches in a city together to pray for their locality. When the hearts of leaders are given to intercession, practical overtures for further cooperation will always follow.

There is a key to success in such endeavors. The following is a prophetic word the Lord gave me in 1990 concerning unity between the various streams of believers. It points out this key.

I found myself in a desert where everything was very dry and parched. Then the Lord opened my eyes, and I saw scattered across the face of the desert a large number of streams with the water of life flowing in them. The Lord revealed to me that the desert represents the condition of believers who have become dry and barren in their hearts, and where the Holy Spirit has ceased to flow among them.

However, the Lord said that, in time, one in such a group will recognize the great need to seek Him in repentance and to move forward in the purpose of God. When this happens, the Lord extends grace to this person who by faith will begin to dig a trench in the sand. As he does so, the Holy Spirit fills the trench and a stream of the water of life begins to flow in it. Each stream then takes on an identity that is related to the grace and vision of the one digging.

I knew that each stream represented various bodies and denominations of believers who have pressed on to know the Lord after their local churches had lost the fullness and reality of His life among them. They began to dig streams of renewal and restoration!

As I considered the various streams, I saw that they were often quite different from one another. For example, some were short in length while others were long, and one or two were very long indeed; some were narrow and others were quite wide; some were straight and others displayed numerous bends and changes in direction. The latter were those bodies of believers where traditions and dogma had to be circumvented in digging the stream.

However, all streams appeared to be headed in the same direction, generally running in parallel with one another, but never joining together. I then noticed a few streams that had become so shallow they simply ceased to exist. I also noticed that, in some instances, beside these dry stream beds, a fresh stream had broken forth and was flowing on bearing an identity that appeared to be related to the dry stream.

I decided to walk forward in the direction toward which the streams were flowing. As I went, I saw several streams that had just emerged in the desert.

Finally, I came to a new stream that was different than the others. It was much deeper, and its direction of flow, while forward, was somewhat transverse to the other streams so that eventually each one would intersect it. I also noticed that, unlike other streams, its identity was not related to an individual; it was called **humility.**

I observed that as the many streams eventually flowed into **humility,** *they became united. The*

*result was a **mighty increase in the power
and force of the water of life** as it flowed
forward through the desert.*

*As I looked to see where this new stream was
headed, I saw that it flowed into a great river
that was too deep to ford. This was the river of
life flowing from the throne of God! As the
various streams entered into this river, I realized
each body had totally lost all identity. **Only the
Lord and His Name remained visible.***

Humility is the key in building unity. It is important to recognize that unity is not based on conform-
ity, but on humility and submission in our diversity.
Although it may not be largely evident at the
present time, the Spirit of God has begun to build
networks of trust between leaders whose Christian
backgrounds are quite different. These are men of
stature who the Lord will use to declare His heart
to the Church and to help prepare saints for what
lies ahead.

Power to Wage Warfare

The following verse points clearly to the source of
power all believers need for spiritual warfare:

*—But you shall receive power when the Holy
Spirit has come upon you; and you shall be My
witnesses both in Jerusalem, and in all Judea
and Samaria, and even to the remotest part of
the earth.*

Acts 1:8

We are no different than these early believers;
the only source of power for us to become more like
Jesus and do the work of God is the blessed Holy
Spirit (Ephesians 3:16, 20). He will come and indwell

all who hunger for righteousness, who see their need for power and who will ask for Him in faith.

> *If you then, being evil, know how to give good gifts to your children, how much more shall your heavenly Father* **give the Holy Spirit to those who ask Him?**
>
> Luke 11:13

However, He is to be sought as a Person, not as an experience! I learned this truth when I was baptized in the Spirit. As a new believer, I remember how zealous, well-meaning believers kept exhorting me over a ten-month period to "do this" and "try that" in order to have me speak in tongues. "This is the experience you need," I was assured. In frustration, I made a covenant with the Lord; I would fast for three days. Then, at a scheduled conference, hands would be laid upon me by visiting ministries, and I would be baptized in the Spirit. There was faith in my heart when I went to the conference. At the appropriate time, I answered an altar call and one of the speakers laid his hands on my head. Immediately, I felt what I can only describe as liquid fire, or electricity, start at the tips of my fingers on both hands and move down my arms and into my stomach. It seemed to build up into a ball and then began to come up into my throat and mouth. I was startled to hear someone weeping as if his heart would break. At first, I wondered who it was. Then I realized that the weeping was coming from me, even though I was emotionally unmoved. I found myself unable to stand up; I was drunk in the Spirit! It became very clear to me that I had not received an experience; I had received a Person! Someone had come into my being in a fullness I had never before known. The power of this Person was at

work within me! By nature I am reserved and do not
exhibit emotions easily. Now I understood how the
Spirit is more than supernatural utterance; He comes
to sanctify and empower our whole being, body, soul
and spirit.

It is not only a matter of power to perform, but also
of power to change and become more like Jesus. Paul's
words to Timothy point out this greater dimension of
the Spirit's work within believers.

For God did not give a spirit of fearfulness to us,
*but of **power**, and of **love**, and of **self-control**.*
                                    Second Timothy 1:6, IB

We see that the potential of a Spirit-filled believer
is threefold:

• There is power for ministry.

• There is power to develop the character (love) of
  God.

• There is power to control those flaws in one's
  humanity that would hinder either of the first
  two from coming into fullness. This third aspect
  in particular is where prayer, especially prayer
  in the Spirit, is so important.

If satan can obtain access to any part of our being,
such as our thought life or some improper habit, he
can cripple our ministry. A Spirit-filled life is not
simply exercising a spiritual gift; it is a life that is
being conformed to the life of Christ.

To some, the only credible evidence of a Spirit-
filled life is a demonstration of the power gifts of the
Holy Spirit. However, in his epistle to Ephesus, Paul
specifically identifies four other marks of a Spirit-
filled life (Ephesians 5:18-21).

- *"Speaking to one another* in psalms and hymns and spiritual songs" (i.e., prophetic worship and ministry in the body).

- *"Singing and making melody* with your heart to the Lord" (i.e., personal worship and ministry to the Lord, including our prayer life).

- *"Always giving thanks for all things* in the name of our Lord Jesus Christ to God, even the Father" (i.e., a heart of thankfulness and giving thanks for **all** circumstances, pleasant or otherwise, knowing that God has allowed them into our life, and He will cause them to work together for good if we embrace them). If we are called according to the purpose of God, and our life is fully committed to Him, then **everything** that we face in our walk is there with God's permission (Romans 8:28).

- *"Be subject to one another* in the fear of Christ" (i.e., be knit together in submission and unity with others in the church, recognizing that each one has been placed and is sustained by the same Holy Spirit as we are). Because of Him, we are members of one another and of the same family and we are to move as one body.

These attributes do **not** the replace power gifts of the Holy Spirit; they are to accompany them, so that the Kingdom of God is fully manifest in ministry.

The muscles of one who does not exercise will become weak and flabby. The same principle holds true in the realm of spiritual power. We are not called to develop great stature in power and strength so that we can overcome satan; we will develop strength and power as we overcome the evil one and his works. The first step in this process is to destroy wrong **thought** patterns and bad **habit** patterns in our lives that can become

footholds and fortresses for demonic influence. We
cannot be effective against satan if we allow him to
have any area of control in our life! This is particularly true in the realm of our minds (Romans 12:2).

*—For the weapons of our warfare are not of the
flesh, but divinely powerful for the destruction
of fortresses. We are destroying speculations
and every lofty thing raised up against the
knowledge of God, and we are taking every
thought captive to the obedience of Christ.*
                                Second Corinthians 10:4-5

Often the difficulties, circumstances and opposi-
tions we face have been brought into our life so that
we will recognize and deal with some personal weakness. This is why the Lord allowed Judas to carry the
purse; he was to see his need as a thief and repent.
The very hindrances to their service that believers
confront are often opportunities brought by God to
strengthen them redemptively. Strong winds develop
deep roots. Some of the winds that produced such
strength in Paul are listed in his epistle to Corinth:
much endurance, afflictions, hardships, distresses,
beatings, imprisonments, tumults, labors, sleepless-
ness, hunger and evil report (2 Corinthians 6:4-10).
Can ministries be raised up in the Church for the
conflict of these days apart from such winds? I think
not.

The Power to Come

As the Church moves through the decade of the
nineties, I believe she will begin to experience a
greater dimension of the power of God. We are already in a period of growing evangelism that began
in the eighties, especially during the last half of that
decade. We are entering a time of great grace: grace

for repentance and cleansing in the house of God, grace for power evangelism and spiritual warfare, grace for the gospel of the Kingdom to be preached as a witness to all nations resulting in great multitudes being saved, and grace for holiness and glory to rest upon the Church. There will be instances when entire cities or areas will turn to God. This will happen when the "strong man" over that place has been cast down. It will be a final, great manifestation of God's love and grace before His judgment falls on the earth. Governments are being quickly changed and new leaders put into place to prepare the nations for these things.

However, not only nations, but the Church also must undergo change in preparation for the power to come. God is especially calling His people today to intercessory prayer, first for themselves, and then for their nation. To be fruitful in such prayer, it is important for us to identify with the sins of our country. We repent for these sins just as if we were personally guilty of them. This is the heart attitude that will bring us to godly sorrow and repentance which will open the way for grace and revival. A good example is the intercessory prayer of Daniel (Daniel 9).

A particularly important ministry of prayer today is for church leaders in a locality to come together and intercede for their city. As hearts are united in burden and vision, the Lord can raise up a godly eldership over the city and thwart the schemes of satan.

It will be a time when the Lord judges all those who profess His name. Everyone will be tested. The Lord will even use the great web of deception satan is preparing in the New Age Movement for this purpose. All things are under His control.

The Lord has made everything for its [His] own purpose, even the wicked for the day of evil.

Proverbs 16:4

Those whose hearts are not truly given to Him will fall away; the tares will be gathered out from among the good grain. All who practice lawlessness and all stumbling blocks will be gathered out of the Church. Concerning these days, Scripture states that many will fall away and will deliver up one another and hate one another. Many will be misled by false prophets and, because of increased lawlessness, many people's love will grow cold. On the other hand, many of the poor, the oppressed, and those in bondage to drugs and false ideologies (especially in third world nations) will be swept into the Kingdom by a mighty wave of power evangelism (Joel 2:28-32, 3:14). There will be great need for endurance as persecution, lawlessness and deception increases. However, there will be **no lack of God's power** for those in His army who leave their cloisters and go out to seek and save the lost. Great unity will mark those engaged in this task.

The Charismatic Renewal appears to have been a possible fulfillment of Ezekiel 37:2-8. The Holy Spirit was poured out upon many dry, scattered bones, both individuals and churches. There was a great deal of noise and commotion as the word of God came forth in prophecy and teaching. Believers became conscious of their place in the body of Christ. Body ministry and relationship became important, but there was little impact on the harvest fields or the forces of evil. However, in verses 9 and 10, the Lord speaks to the Spirit to breathe upon the body, which then comes to life as an exceedingly great army. I believe this pictures the move of God that the Church is now beginning to experience. The army of the Lord is being raised up (Joel 2:1-11). It is time for the eleventh hour laborers to be sent forth !

CHAPTER FIVE

Releasing
God's Men and Money

The Grace of Giving

All that we have ever received pertaining to life has come to us through the gift of God's love and grace. At creation, God gave man identity, intelligence, a free will, fellowship with Himself and authority to represent Him in ruling the earth.

After Adam's fall, God established a covenant with mankind through Abraham. The Lord later fulfilled His part of this covenant when He freely gave Himself up in death on a cross, in order to offer us forgiveness of our sins and the privilege of regaining eternal life and fellowship with Him. Those who respond in faith are given His Holy spirit, made a member of His body and given a commission to proclaim the gospel of His Kingdom to **every** nation on earth! They are no longer their own; they have been bought with a price to serve Him. Every spiritual blessing comes to us on the basis of His grace—grace that flows out of His covenant.

All that pertains to giving and receiving from God is based on the covenant He has made. This covenant was initiated and established with Abraham, who God declared to be the father of **all** who would afterward become His children. This covenant, which is based on faith, continued to exist even after the covenant of law was given to Israel (Galatians 3:17). It was later confirmed and fulfilled in Christ and became the basis of God's grace and blessing coming to **all** who receive His Son as their Lord and Savior (Galatians 3:8, 14, 22).

A covenant is a **binding** agreement between two parties with **clearly defined** responsibilities and commitments. If one party comes to a place of need, the resources of the second person are to be made available to meet that need.

Today the Church faces the tremendous challenge of a great end-time harvest and spiritual warfare that will close this age. It is imperative that she embrace the covenant principles of **grace and giving** that will ensure the supply of **all** resources necessary for this task. To understand these principles, let us examine the history of our covenant with the Lord, starting with Abraham.

The Abrahamic Covenant

The history of God's dealing in the life of Abraham over many years reveals how covenant commitment was progressively developed in his relationship with the Lord (Genesis 12-22).

The first step began with God making significant promises to Abram. The only condition placed on Abram at this time was that he leave the pagan country he was living in and go to a new land, which he immediately did, an act that required faith (Genesis 12:1-4).

The next event occurred after Abram had rescued his nephew, Lot, from pagan kings. On the way home, the Lord, as Melchizedek, met Abram and blessed him. In response, Abram paid tithes to Him (Genesis 14:17-20).

The third incident took place when the Lord promised personally to be a shield to Abram and to reward him greatly. In response, Abram asked the Lord for a son. God then promised him seed as numerous as stars in the heaven. Because Abram believed this promise, God reckoned his faith as righteousness. On the basis of this faith, God made a covenant promise to give specific areas of land to Abram and his promised descendants (Genesis 13).

The next episode in the process came to pass after a carnal attempt by Abram to have a son by the maid Hagar. The Lord came and reaffirmed His promise that Abram would become a father of "a multitude of nations." However, more was now required of him; he was to change his name to Abraham and to take in his body the pain and mark of physical circumcision as a sign of the covenant he had entered into with God (Romans 4:11). The Lord then said that He would visit Sarah and she would give birth to the promised son of the covenant within a year, which came to pass when her son Isaac was born.

The final step in the process consisted of God's testing Abraham's level of commitment to their covenant. He was asked to offer up the **most precious possession** he had—to sacrifice his son, Isaac! It was Abraham's immediate, unquestioning obedience to do so that proved his total commitment to their covenant (Genesis 22:16-18). The fact that God did not take Isaac's life is unimportant; it was Abraham's willingness to give him up that made it clear he recognized that all he possessed belonged to God.

We can learn much from this history of our spiritual father. It is good to believe the gospel and be saved. However, we are called to a higher plane: to recognize that **everything we own, and all that we are,** belong to the Lord. In the covenant of grace, God has given to us His most precious possession, the Lord Jesus. He has promised to meet all of our needs; in return, we are to acknowledge that all we have and are belongs to Him. Furthermore, it is not only a matter of spiritual blessings. God tells us that He owns all gold, silver and precious stones; all livestock belongs to Him. Thus, covenant with the Lord addresses **everything** we will ever need!

Let us next examine God's covenant relationship with Israel to gain additional insight on giving and receiving.

The Covenant of Moses and God's House

The covenant God made with Israel through Moses reveals new understanding of the grace of giving to the Lord. In this particular covenant, the house of God was introduced with specific laws put in place by the Lord for its construction and maintenance as well as support of the priesthood who served Him in the house. In addition, the Lord established provision to support the poor among the people.

These laws of giving were as follows:

- The Tabernacle was to be **built** with the free will **offerings** of the people (Exodus 25:1-8, 35:21).

- The Tabernacle was to be **maintained and restored with offerings** from the people (Exodus 30:12-16, 2 Chronicles 24:4-10, Nehemiah 10:31-39).

- The Levites who served in His house were to be **supported by tithes** from the people. The

Levites were to pay a tithe on their tithes to the high priest (Numbers 18:21-28). Tithing was an **obligation.** The Lord declared that the tithe belonged **to Him** and was therefore holy (Leviticus 27:30). The Law did **not** introduce tithing; it endorsed and made mandatory what was begun by Abraham and carried on by his descendants (Genesis 28:22).

- Every third year, the tithe of all produce from the fields was to be shared between the Levites, the aliens, the orphans and the widows (Deuteronomy 14:22, 27-29). The Lord's instruction to Israel was to show mercy by helping the poor and needy (Is. 58:6-7). The corners of the harvest fields, the gleanings of the field and vineyards were to be left for the needy and the stranger (Leviticus 19:9-10).

God's word to Israel was **absolutely clear** in requiring the nation to support His work through **two** distinct methods of giving: tithes and offerings.

"Will a man rob God? Yet you are robbing Me! But you say, 'How have we robbed Thee?' In **tithes and offerings.** *You are cursed with a curse, for you are robbing Me, the whole nation of you! Bring the* **whole tithe** *into the storehouse so that there may be food in My house, and test Me now in this,— says the Lord of hosts, —if I will not open for you the windows of heaven, and pour out for you a blessing until it overflows."*

Malachi 3:8-10

The bottom line in the Lord's words are two options: obedience in tithes and offerings, with the promised blessing of abundance, or disobedience, with the curse of poverty.

From these two covenants as His people, we learn that to receive all of the Lord's blessings, we must be as totally committed as He is to the covenant which binds us together. It may indeed have been initiated by His grace, but both parties are bound by the covenant.

To further establish our understanding of this subject, let us examine the covenant relationship that existed between the early Church and the Lord.

The Early Church

There are essentially six observations that mark how the early Church addressed their stewardship of giving.

- The depths of commitment in these first century saints was demonstrated in that they **first gave themselves to the Lord,** and then they brought their material offerings (2 Corinthians 8:5). This does not mean that one should not tithe or give offerings until he is perfect in heart, but that as we prepare to give, we should repent of withholding any area of our lives from the Lord.

- Believers saw themselves as stewards of **all** that they possessed, and great grace was upon them as they shared their possessions with those who had need (Acts 2:44-47, 2 Corinthians 8:1-14).

- Local and translocal ministries were supported by the saints, most likely through tithes (Romans 10:13-15, Galatians 6:6). These men saw themselves as **working for the Lord** as His representatives, **not** as employed by the church. Paul set a personal example for leaders by often supporting himself through secular work in order to demonstrate the covenant principle that it is more blessed to give than to receive (Acts 20:33-35).

- Ministry to the poor was a common and shared burden of the apostles (Galatians 2:10). Their concern was imparted to the saints and generously supported by them (2 Corinthians 8, 9). The handling of all offerings was placed in the hands of men with proven integrity and accountability (Acts 11:27-30, 1 Corinthians 16:1-4, 2 Corinthians 8:16-24). The motivation to give, imparted to the saints by the apostles, was not simply to meet needs, but that the grace of their giving would bring much glory and thanksgiving to the Lord. They were, in effect, giving to Him, and He would greatly bless them in return so that they would have even more to give (2 Corinthians 9:7-14).

- There is **no** mention of support for church buildings. During the lifetime of the first apostles, the church was located in homes. Where possible, synagogues were used to evangelize while the church was built in homes, where the primary emphasis was on the spiritual house of the Lord, the body of Christ (Acts 2:46, Romans 16:5, 1 Corinthians 16:19, Col. 4:15, Acts 18:7-8, 11).

- No resources were used to support para-church functions; **all** ministry was an expression **local church** life and oversight.

What Can Today's Church Learn from this History?

The issues of giving and resource-need can only be properly understood within the context of the Lord's covenant for a particular time. In the day of Abraham, the covenant at the time was centered in a family and, in particular, a son:

Isaac. The only resources of concern were those of Abraham's family. What Abraham was unable to supply, God provided through the supernatural birth of Isaac.

In the day of Moses, the covenant concerned a **nation** who God promised to dwell among if they would obey and serve Him. Now there was a greater need for resources: construction and maintenance of the Lord's house; support of the priesthood; and care for the poor and needy of the nation.

However, the covenant with the Church today concerns the **whole world!** She is commissioned to preach the gospel of the Kingdom to **every** nation, with an emphasis on ministering to the poor. The resources now required are **infinitely** greater! This task **cannot possibly** be carried out apart from the supply of God; only the Lord can accomplish such a work! However, He will not do it apart from His people, who are stewards of His resources. The proper focus and emphasis is not on novel methods to raise money; it is faith in the Lord to supply. Everything belongs to Him; He can shake nations, or simply touch the heart of a wealthy man to release resources into His purpose.

> *"And I will shake all the nations; and they will come with the wealth of all nations; and I will fill this house with glory," says the Lord of hosts. "The silver is Mine, and the gold is Mine," declares the Lord of hosts.*
>
> Haggai 2:7-8

The following observations from the Word of God and the three periods of His covenant with His people provide basic, **vital** principles by which resource-needs facing the Church today can be met.

- The story of Abraham reveals that one who has **wholly** given himself to God will not withhold his most precious possession from Him. This was also the heart attitude of saints in the early Church, and it must also become ours as well. The two key factors in the Abrahamic covenant were the **faith** of Abraham to believe and give and the **grace** of God to supply what **only He could do.** The task facing the Church today is just as impossible as was Sarah's pregnancy; it **can only be accomplished by the power of God!** Our responsibility is to believe, to give ourselves wholly to Him, and He will do what we cannot do! As stewards, we have two primary responsibilities. First, we are not to covet things for ourself; we are to pass them on quickly. Second, we are to be a clean conduit for the flow of God's resources to others. We are to plan well, to be diligent and to move in faith. Above all, we are to recognize that the Lord is the Source of our supply. Regardless of how well we do, it is the Lord who supplies. Natural methods of supply are subject to natural influences such as recession, drought, business failure or earthquakes. However, Jehovah-Jireh is totally unaffected by economic factors.

- God's Word is clear: one who practices sin is a slave to sin. Indeed, whatever has control over us enslaves us. Because of our covenant to God, we belong only to Him. Thus, when believers take upon themselves a debt that controls them, they greatly hinder their covenant position with the Lord and weaken His promises of supply to them. In the Old Testament, there was provision to forgive debts every seven years (Deuteronomy 31:10). The Lord's prayer in the New Testament contains these words:

*And forgive us our debts, as we also have for-
given our debtors.*

Matthew 6:12

The Old Testament speaks to this principle as well:

*The rich rules over the poor, and the borrower
becomes the lender's slave.*

Proverbs 22:7

The best way to be sure of being without debts is
not to create any in the first place.

*Owe nothing to anyone except to love one
another —.*

Romans 13:8a

Credit can be a valuable servant, but it can also be
a terrible task master. Our nation today is strangling
under a suffocating load of debt. This is true on personal, corporate and national levels. The economy is
sure to eventually collapse like a house built of straw.
Deficit financing is as contrary to the Kingdom of God
as communism is. The issue is clear: for the church to
have sufficient resources for her God-ordained ministry, she cannot be in bondage to debt. While this is
true for congregations, it is even more important for
individual families. The answer is simple: Get out of
debt! If we are to be good stewards of the Lord's
resources, our investment of them should be in tangible assets and not in paper backed by excessive debt.
It is difficult to estimate the amount of tithe money
that goes to pay interest on mortgages by churches in
America! This is **not** what God intends the tithe to be
used for. A church should have a mortgage only if it
serves the purpose of God and does not curtail ministry.

For over thirty years, my wife and I have bought
nothing unless we could pay cash for it. The one

exception has been our homes, which have tangible worth.

- The history of Israel makes it clear that being **obligated by law** to tithe and give can **never** take the place of freely giving out of love and commitment to the Lord. If God doesn't have our hearts, then our tithes and offerings will not meet the mark. They may benefit others, but we will walk in spiritual poverty. The key is the grace of giving, and we cannot do this as we should if our heart is centered on gaining wealth and possessions for ourselves. We will prosper as we give to others (Proverbs 4:24-25).

And God is able to make all grace abound to you, that always having all sufficiency in everything, you may have an abundance for every good deed.
                                      Second Corinthians 9:8

- The **first and most important** use of tithes in the church is to support those who minister the Word of God. The priority is men, not buildings! It is important that young men being raised up for ministry in the generation ahead be trained with trades, skills and professions that are easily mobile so that, like Paul, they may have "tent-making" capabilities to support themselves when necessary.[9] Men who are called into one of the fivefold ministries of Ephesians 4:11 should divorce themselves from the traditional mindset of becoming "professional clergy." Jesus wants to be Lord over **every** aspect of their life, whether secular or spiritual; indeed, when we serve the Lord we find that our whole life is spiritual. Some of these men He will call into trades or professions where skills and qualities of their manhood, prepared in the womb of their mothers, will be developed and used to generate resources to support them in His service. These would minister on a part-time basis. Other men will be called to spend "full time" in ministry. Still others will minister on a part-time basis while also being blessed by God to creatively raise up businesses in order to generate resources and provide employment for other believers. Every minister should be willing to work and support himself if the need to do so arises. The Church should reorient its thinking relative to finances. Some large building programs of the past have arisen out of the ambitions of man rather than the purpose of God; the result has been a burden of debt on the saints with a corresponding lack of support for the gospel of the Kingdom. The following is a partial listing of trades, professions and businesses that can provide "tent-making" support and generate resources.

PROFESSIONS	
Nurse	Lawyer
Physician	Optometrist
Dentist	Teacher
Pharmacist	Programmer
Engineer	Chemist
Attorney	Consultant
Accountant	Translator
TRADES	
Optician	Medical/Dental Technician
Carpentry	Repair Services
Electrician	Barber/Hairdresser
Sales	Motor Mechanic
Toolmaking	Clerical Work
Surveyor	Draftsman
Plumbing	Secretary
Janitor	Refrigeration

BUSINESSES	
Crafts	Print Shop
Tutoring	Photography
Cottage Industry	Agriculture
Publication	Entrepreneur (Invest- ments)
Manufacturing	Water Treatment
Cleaning Services	Contractor

- A proper focus in preaching the gospel is reaching out to the poor and afflicted. This emphasis will demand greater resources, which will be supplied as the grace of giving is developed in the saints. This emphasis should be present in every assembly. Very often the key resource is not money; it can be simply a willingness to give up some of our time to go out and take the gospel to those in need. It can also be sharing one's home as a place of shelter and supply to a person who is homeless. To deny ourselves in such ways is to give to the Lord (Matthew 25:34-40). Each child of God is called to help the poor. If we wait to accumulate a supply over and above our needs before we minister to the poor, we may never start. We are to move in faith that our supply is in the Lord; He will provide, for He is Jehovah-Jireh!

He who gives to the poor will never want, but he who shuts his eyes will have many curses.

Proverbs 28:27

- Today, because of the **immense** scope of ministry, there exist needs for resources to support many functions that did not concern the first church (e.g., communications, technology, travel, materials). In general, such needs should be met with our **offerings.** Each local church needs to know and promote God's vision and purpose for them as an assembly and to give accordingly.

- The handling of **all** monies in ministry must be done with godly **integrity** and **accountability** both in the church and in the eyes of the world.

- Giving should be systematic (1 Corinthians 16:1-2). Legalism, coercion or constant asking for money should be avoided. The motive and messages of leaders are always to be centered in seeking God's perfect will for the people, not seeking what they possess (2 Corinthians 12:14-15). However, there must be clear instructions to the saints of the blessings contained in Scriptures such as the following:

Give, and it will be given to you; good measure, pressed down, shaken together, running over, they will pour into your lap. For by your standard of measure it will be measured to you in return.

Luke 6:38

There is one who scatters, yet increases all the more, and there is one who withholds what is justly due, but it results only in want. The generous man will be prosperous, and he who waters will himself be watered.

Proverbs 11:24-25

Support of Translocal Ministry

The Church would die if her only emphasis was the excellence of local ministry; she must bring forth and release translocal ministries who are equipped to fulfill the purpose of God. These ministries become an extension of the local church that released them to travel. The fathering of churches is the responsibility of apostolic team ministry. Three basic principles of translocal ministry can be seen in the record of Paul and Barnabas who were sent out from the church at Antioch.

*—The **Holy Spirit said,** "Set apart for Me Barnabas and Saul for the work to which I have called them." Then, when they had fasted and prayed and laid their hands on them, they sent them away. So, **being sent out by the Holy Spirit**—*

Acts 13:2b-4a

The Holy Spirit sent them, while the church released them. The ones sent were experienced apostolic men who had grace to lay church foundations. The key verb is "send"; they were not "let go," but "sent."

- There was an accountability required of those sent.

*—They sailed to Antioch, from which they had been commended to the grace of God for the work that they had accomplished. And when they had arrived and gathered the **church** together, they began to report all things that God had done with them—.*

Acts 14:26-27

- There was a recognized responsibility of local churches to support translocal ministry.

*Beloved, you are acting faithfully in whatever you accomplish for the brethren, and especially when they are strangers; and they bear witness to your love before the church; and you will do well **to send them** on their way in a manner worthy of God. For they went out for the sake of the Name [not in the name of an organization], accepting nothing from the Gentiles. Therefore* *we ought to support such men, that we may be fellow workers with the truth.*

Third John 5-8

A study of Paul's subsequent translocal ministry supports these principles and provides further insight into how the church today should operate. For example, Paul always depended upon God's grace. Whether there was financial support or not, he labored, never requiring or expecting support from those he ministered to. He frequently worked with his hands (e.g., at Ephesus)

- **The example Paul set at Corinth (A.D. 52/53)**
  Writing in A.D. 56, three to four years after he founded the church at Corinth, Paul says:

If we sowed [past tense] spiritual things in you, is it too much if we should [lit., shall; future tense] reap material things from you? — Nevertheless, we did not [past tense] use this right.

First Corinthians 9:11-12

Paul clearly states his expectations of support in the **future** for what he had done in the **past.**

*But I shall come to you after I go through Macedonia, for I am going through Macedonia; and perhaps I shall stay with you, or even spend the winter, **that you may send me on my way** wherever I may go.*

First Corinthians 16:5-6

Furthermore, Paul always ministered as part of a team, and he expected support for team members. He speaks for Timothy, who was on his team:

Now if Timothy comes, see that he is with you without cause to be afraid; for he is doing the Lord's work, as I also am [i.e. translocal ministry]. Let no one therefore despise him.

But send him on his way in peace, so that he may come to me; for I expect him with the brethren.

First Corinthians 16:10-11

In his epistle to Corinth Paul reveals how he was supported initially when the Corinthians themselves failed to follow through with support:

And I rejoice over the coming of Stephanas and Fortunatus and Achaicus; because they have supplied what was lacking on your part.

First Corinthians 16:17

Paul expands on this principle in his second epistle, approximately one year later.

Or did I commit a sin in humbling myself that you might be exalted, because I preached the gospel of God to you without charge? I robbed other churches, taking wages from them to serve you; and when I was present with you and was in need, I was not a burden to anyone; for when the brethren came from Macedonia, they fully supplied my need—.

Second Corinthians 11:7-9

Here we see that Macedonian churches supported Paul in his ministry at Corinth. Paul expressed his expectation of future support from the Corinthian church:

And in this confidence I intended to at first to come to you, that you might twice receive a blessing; that is, to pass your way into Macedonia, and again from Macedonia to come to you, and by you to be helped [i.e., sent]) on my journey to Judea.

Second Corinthians 1:15-16

- **The example of Paul's ministry at Rome**
  This epistle was written (A.D. 57/58) in **anticipation** of his coming to Rome:

But now, with no further place for me in these regions [around Greece], and since I have had for many years a longing to come to you whenever I go to Spain for I hope to see you in passing, and to be helped [i.e., sent] on my way there by you—.

Romans 15:23-24

- **The example of Paul's ministry at Phillipi**
  In his epistle to Philippi, written in A.D. 60, nine to ten years after he first ministered to the believers there, Paul says:

But I rejoiced in the Lord greatly, that now at last you have revived your concern for me; indeed, you were concerned before, but you lacked opportunity. Not that I speak from want; for I have learned to be content in whatever circumstances I am. —Nevertheless, you have done well to share with me in my affliction. And you yourselves also know, Philippians, that at the first preaching of the gospel, after I departed from Macedonia, no church shared with me in the matter of giving and receiving but you alone; for even in Thessalonica you sent a gift more than once for my needs.

Philippians 4:10-16

It is clear that the Philippian church supported Paul after he left them in Macedonia and went to Thessalonica, just as the Macedonian churches had supported him in his first ministry at Corinth.

We can conclude that **every** church Paul laid foundations for, whether they could support him initially or not, was expected to support his translocal ministry in the future. Their support did not die out in time; the Philippian church continued their support ten years after he first came to them.

Thus translocal support is based on the **spiritual fruit** of foundational ministry at churches established or strengthened by a minister. Good foundational ministries are to be supported in a systematic manner by assemblies who have been helped by them so that the church **overall** may be extended in the Lord's purpose.

The integrity of a translocal ministry in the eyes of those who support it is exemplified in Paul's ministry by a willingness to work with his hands when necessary (Acts 20:17-35), as well as his godly counsel and practice concerning the receiving and handling of offerings.

From this study of Paul's traveling ministry and the churches he established, we can make four observations that provide guidelines for churches today.

- Every assembly should have a **vision** to **raise up and release** translocal ministries to plant new churches, and they should be willing to support such ministry when it travels to the wider body.

- Local churches need the input of translocal ministries so that their saints can be properly equipped for service. To the extent they are able, they are to financially support such ministry both at the time and in the future. If there is little or no support available, these ministries should still come to minister, being willing to work with their hands or to receive support from other churches that they are in relationship with.

- Every minister must hear the heart of God concerning how he is to be supported, whether by others or by his own work. He must always be accountable in his handling of finances.

- Churches must break free from the tradition of having one or two paid professional ministers care for the saints. An assembly is called by God to be a local expression of the body of Christ in which each member is equipped for a specific place of service. There should be a growing number of elders providing shepherding and equipping functions, many of whom will support themselves by secular work or businesses. The tithe should be used only for the support of ministers; offerings would provide support for other needs such as buildings. When churches embrace Kingdom principles and return to the pattern of the early Church, there should be no shortage of resources.

The release and support of translocal ministries is not primarily a matter of rules and procedure; it is one of relationship between the ministers and the churches they have input to. The gospel of the Kingdom does not require a class of "super ministers"; the Lord seeks ordinary men whom He has called and who have become bonded together in a united commitment to His purpose. The resources needed to support them lies in the stewardship of each believer and in the grace and supply of God. Our individual stewardship includes talents, skills, industry and creativity as well as our anointing, money and time. To every believer in each church the Lord says,

Give yourselves wholly to Me. Be faithful in tithes and offerings and I will develop the grace

of giving in you and bring blessing into your lives. Those things you cannot supply, I will provide; and the greater your need, the greater will be My provision.

Conclusion

Someone recently asked me what I see ahead for the Church. My reply was "Change, change and more change!" The following are some areas in which I expect significant changes to take place as the purpose of God unfolds for the days ahead.

- There is going to be a greater emphasis on ministry to the poor. The world is tired of hearing "words on religion"; people are looking for reality. They want to see truth in action, in the life as well as the message of preachers. People are looking for answers to the great and growing problems that are enveloping society all over the world. The answer to **all** needs is the Lord Jesus Himself. He is calling His people to pay the price of commitment, to throw off the mantle of apathy, and to take the gospel of the Kingdom to the streets. He wants to reach out through hearts filled with compassion and mercy, and through hands extended to the poor, the crippled and the homeless. The word of the Lord to churches is to take down their walls of isolation and go out together into their communities to redeem the poor and afflicted and bring them into His house.

• The Church will become more relevant to society. To combat the growing thrust of the New Age Movement, we need to pray for God to raise up leaders like Joseph and Daniel into places of influence and authority in the land. Daniel was a prophetic voice of righteousness and deliverance to his nation. Joseph was a righteous implement of deliverance for his people. Both are needed today in our nation, and I believe God will raise up such men from within the Church. For example, God may raise up a man to whom the nation would listen, declaring that repentance, not vaccine, is needed to stem the A.I.D.s plague. The growing harvest of souls in South America will eventually result in positive changes for good in the economic and spiritual life of the nations affected, and this will involve men of great stature.

• Evangelism will become established in churches which today operate in a maintenance rather than growth mode. The gospel of the Kingdom cannot be separated from the life, government and vision of a local church, for both are necessary to fulfill the purpose of God. The Lord is investing His very best in the gospel with which He will bring this age to a close. To participate, His people must be willing to lay down their lives and all they possess to sow into this great task. Churches require a new vision of how the Lord will provide resources for the work of His harvest and how to be good stewards of what He will release to them. Traditional methods will not be adequate for the harvest ahead.

- The Lord is judging and purging His people, especially leaders, to prepare the Church for the future. Bonds that hold her to the world are being broken. There will be an exodus of the uncommitted, of tares and stumbling blocks, from those churches that move in the purpose of God. The goals and structures devised over centuries where the control of man—authority based on offices or hierarchical government—will be shaken by the Lord; religious kingdoms that promote man's control will begin to fail. Two things that cannot exist together in a church are new wine and old wine skins! Biblical order and the spontaneity of body life will grow in local churches. The centrality of Jesus will become the most important emphasis in the Church. The ministry of apostles and prophets will again become commonplace. Integrity and accountability will become primary credentials of valid ministry.

- The Church is being mobilized as a mighty army of the Spirit to bring back to the Kingdom of God what satan has usurped. New dimensions of worship, praise, spiritual gifts and ministries will be brought forth to demonstrate the power of God and to overcome the forces of evil. The vision of the Lord will be made clear through prophetic ministry so that His army will move as one man. The Lord will raise up peacemakers whom He will use to network various streams of believers together in service. As churches embrace what the Lord is doing, much of what contributes to division today in the body of Christ will cease to exist. The issue is not doctrine, but the government of God. The very conditions of distress (national calamities, economics, persecution) will serve to draw churches together. The Kingdom of God will be established in the Church!

- There will be a growing consciousness in the Church of the voice of the Bridegroom calling His bride to prepare. The return of the Lord is probably more related to the state of the bride than it is to conditions in the world. This ministry of the Holy Spirit will continue until **all** enemies are under His feet and the Lord Jesus has come to have **first place** in everything in His Church. At that time, the bride of Christ will have made herself ready. Our eyes will become more focused upon Him than on ministry or ourselves. There will be a greater clarity of His final purpose when He will dwell among His people in the holy city, the New Jerusalem, His chosen place of rest. This **future center of the Kingdom** from which His government will go forth to all creation, the Zion of God, will be made up of the overcomers from among His people. They will be those who have fully come under His government and who have been conformed into the image of Jesus. All creation is eagerly awaiting this unveiling of God's sons, which will be a climactic consequence of the preaching of the gospel of the Kingdom (Romans 8:18-23).

- Finally, if we believe all these thing to be true, if we have insight into the strategy of the Lord and understand the great needs that now exist in the Church, what is the first thing we should do? I believe the answer is intercession! I expect the importance and practice of prayer to grow and become pervasive throughout the Church. Like Daniel, we must identify with the sins and failures of our country and the Church. Our sorrow and repentance should be as great as the most guilty person; our heart ought to be broken for sin just as our Lord's heart is. This is the manner in which we identify with His burden and work in these days.

Having expressed my heart, I close this book with a prophetic word given to a gathering of ministers. This message was delivered by Bob Meares, a prophetic brother from Laconia, New Hampshire. I consider it to be a valid word from the Lord for the Church today.

I have gathered you together in these conferences to announce a new thing I am doing in the earth. I proclaimed last year the coming of age of a new generation of servants who are to lead My people in a new way.

I raise up a new generation because the thing I am doing is too new, too different from what has been, to entrust the vision to minds and hearts already filled with the visions of the past. And so I have chosen you as new parchment on which to write a new word, on which to sketch a new vision.

Hear then the word and see the vision: The great linchpin in the midst of the sea has been unfastened, releasing the waves of the sea to roar and pitch as if out of control. Last year it was done. The ancient lock, which no man could break, was opened and the bonds that held the Church and the world together were loosened, never to be joined again.

This year I cause a mighty bell to sound, signaling the demolition of the structures that have accommodated the godly and the ungodly in an unholy alliance in the name of worship and church. I have brought you to a great continental divide in the spirit, separating one epoch of history from another, changing the patterns of centuries. Therefore you must prepare my people for a time unlike anything you have known. Build as Noah built — not for the times he knew or the conditions he experienced, but for unheard of times and conditions that had never been before and would never be again.

The plans and directions are already in your hands, but you have not seen them as they are. Look into the Scriptures with new eyes and open hearts. From this day forth I will cause you to see wonderful things that you do not know. I will unlock to you the Sermon on the Mount, the Olivet Discourse, the words given to the sons of Zebedee and Peter. But build like the wise men who dig deep and build their houses on the rock. For be assured, the storms will come, wild and terrible, and only those will stand who build solidly.

Understand this: You must divorce yourselves from a tradition that rejoices in learning but not in doing, that is content to hear and will not obey.

*"And this **gospel of the kingdom** shall be preached in the whole world for a witness to all nations, **and then the end shall come!**"*

Bibliography

1. R.J. Dake, *God's Plan for Man;* Dake Bible Sales, P.O. Box 1050, Lawrenceville, GA 30246; 1987.

2. Dr. I.D.E. Thomas, *The Omega Conspiracy;* Growth Publishing, P.O. Box 661, Herndon, VA 22070; 1986.

3. D.H. Rumble, *The Crucible of the Future;* Destiny Image, P.O. Box 310, Shippensburg, PA 17257; 1989.

4. D.H. Rumble, *Prepared for His Glory;* Destiny Image, P.O. Box 310, Shippensburg, PA 17257; 1986.

5. D. MacPherson, *The Incredible Cover-up;* Omega Publications, P.O. Box 4130, Medford, OR 97501; 1980.

6. Dan Juster and Keith Intrater, *Israel, the Church and the Last Days;* Destiny Image, P.O. Box 310, Shippensburg, PA 17257; 1990.

7. G.E. Ladd, *The Last Things;* Wm. B. Eerdmans, 255 Jefferson Ave. SE, Grand Rapids, MI 49503; 1979.

8. R.N. Baer, *Inside the New Age Nightmare;* Huntington House, P.O. Box 53788, Lafayette, LA 78505; 1989.

9. L. Peabody, *Secular Work Is Full-time Service;* Christian Literature Crusade, Fort Washington, PA 19034; 1988

Crucible of the Future by Dale Rumble. Here is an incredible look into the 1990's by a former IBM futurist. In this book, the author turns his attention to the world of the future as it relates to the Church's triumphant but costly role in the last generation of this age. The Church will face the most challenging test ever of her devotion to the Lord, her purity and her real supernatural power. It is a glorious picture of restoration in the mist of international turmoil. TPB-168 p. ISBN 0-914903-89-6 Retail $6.96

Prepared for His Glory by Dale Rumble. What is it that really prepares a man for God's glory? In this book, Dale Rumble gives us a fresh view of what God is doing in the Church, as well as what lies ahead for His people. God's intention is for His glory to be intricately woven into the fabric of who we are as men and women. This is expressed simply in words and vivid graphic illustrations. This is a foundational and preparatory manual for this generation of Christians who will abandon all to follow Christ. TBP-288 p. ISBN 0-914903-08-X Retail $8.95

Winds of Change by Donald Rumble. "The greatest mistake," wrote A. W. Tozer, "is to resist change." Nonetheless, such resistance appears endemic to human nature. This booklet was written to challenge believers to respond to the Lord in these critical times of change. A whole new realm of spiritual life and truth awaits all who will be truly open to God's moving, as He leads us to change from one degree of glory to another. PB-72 p. ISBN 0-914903-12-8 Retail $2.95

The Ephesian Connection by Donald Rumble. This book is a prophetic call for God's people to make the connection! The Ephesian Connection begins with heart-felt repentance and a resolve to live in intimate communion with the Lord Jesus. It is only when this happens that the Church will discover who she really is and will bring to this generation the power of the ages to come. TPB-210 p. ISBN 1-56043-016-8 Retail $5.95

A TIME TO DANCE: AN IN-VITATION by *Barbara Knoll*. The biblical dance is a lifestyle not limited to movement with music, yet such movement is an exciting expression of our worship to the Lord. This is a passionate call for a heart that dances before the Lord, both in movement and in relation-ship to Him. TPB-112 p. ISBN 1-56043-703-0 Retail $5.95

Whatever Happened to the Power of God? by *Dr. Michael L. Brown*. Have you ever wondered why those seriously ill are seldom healed; why people fall in the Spirit, yet remain unchanged; why believers can speak in tongues and wage spiritual warfare without impacting society? This book confronts you with life-changing answers. TPB-210 p. ISBN 1-56043-042-7 Retail $7.95

From the Father's Heart by *Charles Slagle*. This is a beautiful look at the Father's heart. Includes short love notes and letters, as well as prophetic words from God to His children diligently seeking Him. TPB-160 p. ISBN 0-914903-82-9 Retail $6.95

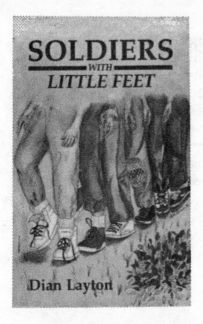

David Worshiped a Living God by *Judson Cornwall*. This is Judson's newest book on praise and worship, destined to become a classic as it describes in beautiful detail the names of God and what they mean to the worshiping saint. TPB-182 p. ISBN 0-938612-38-7 Retail $6.95

Worship as David Lived It by *Judson Cornwall*. This is part two of a trilogy about David's heart and life as a worshiper. This book will show you the intimacy and the necessity of God's nearness as it is discovered in a life of worship. TPB-196 p. ISBN 1-56043-700-6 Retail $6.95

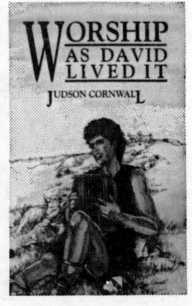